Nothing in this book is to be construed as, or to take the place of, appropriate medical advice, diagnosis or treatment.

D1707086

Published by
Bernard Jensen Enterprises
24360 Old Wagon Road
Escondido, California 92027

*Dedicated to
Art Jensen,
son, friend &
business associate,
all of which
I deeply appreciate.*

CONTENTS

INTRODUCTION 1

Chapter 1. The Chemical Story 17
  Silicon, Calcium, Magnesium & Iron 18
  Herbs for the Body 19
  The Cure Is Not In a Bottle 20
  Go the the Mountains for a High Blood Count 20
  Touch the Greens 20
  All That Touches the Body Goes Into the Body 21
  The Value of an Elimination Diet 21
  Come Up for Air 22
  Artificial Sunlight 23
  Eyeglasses & Ultraviolet 23
  Fluorescent Lights and Vitamin A 24
  Some Extra Health Tips 24

Chapter 2. Catarrh as a Host for Disease 27
  Catarrh 28
  Catarrhal Conditions 30
  Consequences of Suppression 33
  The Four Stages of Disease 34
  Iridology and Catarrh............................. 35
  Elimination of Catarrh 35
  An Ounce of Prevention 37

Chapter 3. Fatigue 39
  Fatigue Cited in Part for Crash 39
  Common Fatigue Procedures 40
  Different Sources of Fatigue...................... 41
  Stages of Fatigue................................. 42
  What Happens in a Tired Body 43
  How Stars and Athletes Fight Fatigue.............. 44

Chapter 4. Mind Over Disease..................... 47
  How Mind Creates and Builds Disease............... 47
  Psychosomatic Disease 47

The Placebo Effect and Healing 50
We Have to "Feel Better" Before We Can Feel Better 52
The Healing Force Within 52
The Healing Power of Harmony 53
Opening to Higher Potentials 55
The Great Within 56
When the Healing Begins 56
Imagination — A Vital Cure Start in Life 58
Aphorisms or Axioms To Believe In 62

Chapter 5.   Vital Force and Vitality Wasters 65

Chapter 6.   Do Drugs Belong in Your Body? 73

Chapter 7.   Taking Care of Your Lymph System 81
The Necessity of the Lymph System 83
Lymph Nourishes and Cleanses the Body 86
The Large Bowel 86
The Lazy Bowel 87
The Proof of the Pudding 88
The Lymph Stream — A Delivery System 90
Correlations with the Lymph Stream and Elimination . . . 90
Convalescent Homes 92
Immunity in the Lymph Stream 96
Now What Do We Do About It? 97
Here Is the Big Lesson 100
We Will Not Get Well with Treatments Alone 100
There Is Much Education Needed 101

Chapter 8.   Understanding the Healing Crisis 103
Drugs and Symptoms 103
Acute, Subacute, Chronic & Degenerative Conditions . . . 104
Constitutional Strength and Inherent Weaknesses 105
Hering's Law of Cure 106
The Healing Crisis 108
After the Healing Crisis 111

Chapter 9.   Self-Suggestion 113
Application of Self-Suggestion 114

LONGEVITY

Methusela lived a thousand years,
As I have often read.
No chemicals were in his soil,
No springs were in his bed.

He did not spray his "tater patch,"
His grapes, or apple trees.
He ate 'em, bugs and all, I guess,
As healthy as you please.

He bought no cake mix full of sin,
He took no coffee breaks,
No cigarettes for his morale,
No aspirin for his aches.

There was no doc to give him shots,
No cokes or cones to buy.
With simplest food he satisfied
His body's full supply.

Now if you'd live a thousand years
You'll likewise have to shun
The poison in your soil and food,
The weiner and the bun;
But I can promise you you'll have
Just years and years of fun.

— Marjorie K. Lawrence

INTRODUCTION

The real voice we have is the one that is silent, expressing itself from within. This little voice on the inside is the one which motivates us to do all that we do. This little voice on the inside is our God within — we each are a spark of God with work to do. We have a responsibility to fulfill God's need by stretching forth and serving that higher calling.

The fulfillment of that responsibility does not mean to attend church on Sunday and forget the spiritual on Monday, Tuesday, Wednesday and the rest of the week until Sunday again. It is the fulfilling of the spiritual, mental and physical on a full-time basis, and it all starts from within.

Do you doubt that inner voice? If I put both a poisoned pickle and a ripe apricot in front of you and ask you to make a choice of which you would like to eat, there is something inside of you which will inspire you to eat the ripe apricot. It tells you that you deserve the very best there is.

Very few people sincerely believe they deserve the very best for themselves because they have been preconditioned to endure hardships, regardless of their own wishes and desires.

Challenges Are Not Hardships

There really are no hardships — anyone who has a good philosophy knows that part of life comprises both challenges and problems. However, challenges and problems do not have to be hardships — even sickness does not have to be a hardship.

I have a friend who told me his best friend was his trouble — it made him alert, made him seek, strive for greater things and helped him develop courage from within. Through his problems, he was driven to accomplish, and through perseverance, he did overcome and met a victory. He had never had a victory until he had something to overcome.

The same holds true for the person who lives in the negative, in fear and pain. He has a dying attitude and a dying altitude. He feels life owes him a living, life is not worthwhile and he wonders what is the use of continuing. He lives in the past — he is doing harm to his body. This negative attitude is bad for his health.

The person who lives in a loving and positive attitude, accepting his responsibilities in life the way he should, will maintain and even improve his health. And it all begins from that voice within. The person who reaches that voice within has begun to start his healing process.

Physically, mentally and spiritually, our bodies need peace and rest. We need serenity and ease of mind. When I speak of serenity and ease of mind, I don't necessarily mean the joyfulness of emotion and excitement which can raise the blood pressure. This emotion can destroy us.

There was a man who bet a few dollars on a horse and won $100. In his exhilarating joy, he broke a blood vessel in his throat, produced a hemorrhage and died! This is not the ecstasy for which we should strive, but serenity and ease of mind.

"I Feel Wonderful"

We have to have complete control over our emotional and mental bodies. What we think and verbalize will come back to us. This is why it is necessary for us to sit down quietly each day, close our eyes and listen to our inner selves for a moment while we say, "I feel wonderful." We have to begin believing it before we can begin our spiritual, mental and physical healing.

Trying to reach that inner voice is the beginning of the spiritual healing. We must do all we can to enhance and draw out the good — which our inner self knows to be true — despite the physical conditioning we have lived with in our lives.

At first our little voices will say, "Oh, no you're not wonderful!" We have been conditioned and trained, through our mortal and physical minds, by television, radio and newspapers to say, "Oh, no, you're not well. You need an aspirin." It is a tremendous challenge to feel wonderful; however, we each have this obligation to our deepest selves to be persistent in our approach toward the positive. We have to feel wonderful, not for the good of others, but for our own good.

I realize this more as I go through life because we are instruments of a million strings. We have been endowed with these instruments to take care of them. As physical beings, we are not free beings — we are continually striving for freedom.

Spiritually speaking, we should only be interested in that which is worthwhile, in that which is good for our fellowmen, recognizing that people are more important than things. We must have a feeling toward one another that is positive. If we cannot help people, we must not hinder them either. There are some people who will not be on the same path we tread or the same level of thinking, and that's okay. Our responsibility is not to others — it is to our own selves we must be true. We must build our strength from within so we know where we are going without. We must reach the place where the quality of anyone else's thinking cannot disturb us, whether it be low or high. "None of this moves me," St. Paul told us.

His Operations Never Touched the Soul

There is such a thing as a divine state. In the divine state, there is no sickness; there is no worry or recuperation necessary. There is no regeneration to take place, because in the divine state, there is no sickness to cure. There is nothing to take care of — no place to go and and nothing to get. We have arrived! We can build this divine state within our own being.

We can't be like the majority of people who go to doctors for their mortal problems. A surgeon friend once told me that he had operated on many people, but he never reached the soul of a person through his operations!

Each person we meet has the same spark within — although we may not see it. The odor and fragrances of flowers did not exist until it first became a reality within you, correct? I am sure you will know the Christ when you see Him and know God, because God is within you. We just haven't gone within to listen to Him through that voice we find deep within.

Next is our mental welfare — are we mentally free? Or are we afraid of the night or tomorrow. Are we afraid there won't be enough money to last? That our insurance is in effect? Have we enough

3

money for rent to pay at the end of the month? These are mental things. They are loads on our shoulders. To tell you a truth, this is a state of being. This is a state of being upset. Why be this way? We must alter the way we think in order to raise our consciousness **and** our health.

A patient of mine wrote to tell me her "coffee story" after she left my Ranch some time ago. She told me how she felt she desperately needed to have some coffee while she was staying at the Ranch and complained about it. "I could get coffee, but I couldn't drink it in front of anybody else and I felt guilty anytime I had it there. I just couldn't wait to get home to get some coffee. I went next door to visit my children, and they were out. I went to a friend's house about a block away and she didn't have any coffee. Then, finally, I walked two miles to a supermarket to get some coffee and when I got home, I couldn't wait until I could drink this cup of coffee. And guess what? It tasted like *dishwater!* This is what happened to me at your Ranch. I got my mind changed, my habits changed and my body changed also, because now I don't particularly care for coffee anymore."

What We Learn from Suffering

We have to change our minds before we change our health. We have to raise our consciousness before we change our health! This again sends us back to my original thought that we must arrive at our own kingdom or divine state — that place within which we can call home — that place within to which we retreat in time of trouble, need, mourning and death. Most of our frustration comes because we don't know there is a better place to live. We don't know how to laugh, don't know where to go and don't know where to find security. The only security is opportunity — the opportunity to change our minds. All the fields are ripe and ready to be harvested if we will just look again. *"Knock and the door shall be opened to you. Seek and ye shall find."*

It is our pain and suffering which offer us our opportunity.

> *"I walked a mile with happy and*
> *she chattered all the way.*
> *She left me none the wiser*
> *for all she had to say.*
> *I walked a mile with suffering and*
> *never a word said she.*
> *But what I learned from suffering,*
> *when suffering walked with me."*

This is when we truly stop, look, and start to listen to that higher self within. This is when we finally say, "Well, now I see." Do you know I've seen people have a new world open up to them the moment they see.

What a shame it would be if there were no one to carry enlightenment or light to people living in dark places. All I can do is carry light hoping that the opportunity will come that my words will help you see a bit better. This is opportunity knocking at the door. And we all are at a level to help someone less knowledgeable than ourselves. This is all we can offer you.

You've got to do it yourselves though. I can't hold you up. You have to hold yourselves up. I'd like to carry you — in fact, when I got out of college, I thought there was a big responsibility put on my shoulders because I was supposed to go around and get people well. I used to pray for people and I worked very hard mentally, physically and spiritually for others. I would give all my patients the best I had. But I realized that you can't give yourself away until people are ready to hear what you have to say.

Everyone must find their own happiness, must learn to live more abundantly, acquire their own knowledge, feel joy and learn how to walk in obedience and discipline.

My Greatest Disappointment

I learned that we cannot carry other people when I experienced the greatest disappointment in my whole life. I learned it early when I first stepped out on the lecture platform. With all sincerity I told my story of nutrition and health — of salads and greens — the beginning of a good life, regeneration and rejuvenation in the body. What happened? The audience "booed" at me. This was the greatest and harshest experience I ever had in my life.

But, whose loss was it? Whose gain was it? I woke up exclaiming, "Is it possible that people don't listen? Is it possible that people can't see?" I found out that everybody is different. "You can lead a horse to water, but you can't make him drink." You can't give yourself away until people are ready.

This is a terrible thing to say, but whan a person wakes up and gets tired of being tired, sick of being sick and bored of being bored, he then becomes ready. When we are ready to throw the old calendar away; we are ready to start the new; we're ready to start a new leaf in life. Every day starts a new day, a new beginning. We must let the dead bury the dead and go on with our lives. Don't wait even until Monday to get rid of the old. When people say to me, "Doctor, whatever you have, I'd like to have," this is the time I can give.

I'm Not Old Enough to Smoke!

If I am offered a cigarette, I say, "I just had one." When he lights up another one ten minutes later and offers me another, I say, "No, I'm not old enough." About the third time, another ten minutes later, he offers me another cigarette. Reluctantly, remembering what I had said and wondering what I am going to say next, when he asks me, "Why don't you smoke?" This is the greatest opportunity that ever comes. I would have missed it if I had made judgments against this person and not handled the first two cigarettes properly. In China they say that advice and salt are two things which should never be given until wanted.

We can't walk around holier than thou. We have to go to the same plane of consciousness of our listeners, if we want to meet them and talk with them. Every psychology or sales class teaches that we should find out what our clients like to do, what their hobbies are. When the arms and barriers are down, the doors are open and salesmen sell their bill of goods.

A lady who had attended my lectures told me of her black servant who always met her at the door with stories of woe, misery—

she constantly complained that this and that was always bad, the day was hardly worthwhile, etc. "I was so intent on getting this servant of mine to change her ways of doing things that I sat down and told her about your lectures saying how wonderful we feel when we don't invite trouble. Don't say anything about your sickness — get rid of sickness! Get it out of your mind!" She went away for a few days and when she came back the servant evidently had done some thinking and met her at the door. The lady said, "Well, how are you Bertha?" She said, "Hell, I'm well; Hell, I'm well!" This was her mental concept of feeling well! She changed her mind and she changed her attitude. She changed her attitude and she changed her health.

"You Make Me Sick To My Stomach"

Our thoughts have much to do with the health of our bodies. A good example is the doctor who observed the stomach of a cat under a fluoroscope and noticed the rate of speed at which it was working. Outside the laboratory a dog barked and the cat's stomach cramped up so that there was no more motion in that stomach for almost three hours. This is true, and I could give you hundreds of other experiences. Haven't we all heard the expression, "You make me sick to my stomach." Could this indeed mean that there is an effect to the stomach? Could the expression, "You give me a pain in the neck," be making chiropractors rich on our mental problems today?

Don't you agree that a lot of your worries just naturally pass away? There are many problems that simply pass away. A friend said that one of the nicest things he found in the Bible was, "And it came to pass. . . ." And it does. Some of our problems appear as mountains which will last forever. A little patience, a little living in a divine state of mind and it will pass.

All that we share with others is for cleansing — physically, mentally and spiritually. If we could just squeeze a sponge in order that we could come out clean physically it would be great. However, we get clean physically by having good foods; we get clean mentally by thinking clean; we become clean spiritually by living spiritually. "Thy sins shall be forgiven thee," we read. God may

7

forgive you your sins, but your nervous system never will. Our mental problems become our physical problems and go down to the base of our fingers.

Thank goodness sickness can pass. Our bodies change and are rejuvenated constantly. Doctors can remove three-quarters of a liver and the liver can rejuvenate itself in seven months' time. The tissue can rejuvenate itself! Have any of you ever cut off the tail of a lizard? Within three months' time, the tail grows back again. This is nature! Nature grows again. Did you ever break off a piece of a little plant and put it in the ground? It grows! Nature wants to build — nature wants to rejuvenate itself.

We Can't Expect Sweet Thoughts with a Sour Stomach

We are nature's children, and we are living in nature. Every 24 hours we make new skin on the palm of our hand. Every hour and a half, all the blood in our bodies goes through the thyroid gland. What does blood do? The life of the body is in the blood. When we have good blood and good circulation of blood, we can rejuvenate the tissues of the body. If we want good toenails, we need good blood, and we need to be able to circulate it. The same is with the hair. So many people are losing their hair by the handfull and they don't know what to do. I learned that the hair is part of our bloodstream — the same as our eyes, nostrils and our thinking. We can't remember well unless we feed our memory centers. We have got to take care of all the mental things physically.

But we simultaneously take care of the physical things mentally. We can't expect sweet thoughts with a sour stomach! By the same token, we can't expect a heart to beat well if we live in fear — it works both ways. We have to find a healthy state mentally and a divine state spiritually.

Perfect health is an ideal — I have never seen it. That is why we must have a goal and a purpose in life towards which to grow. That is why rejuvenation takes place so we can become better. Wouldn't it be a terrible thing if every time we ate a donut, we passed right out? It is possible that some of the good things you do balance the budget a little bit. This is the problem with most people — they go back and forth between health and junk so that they are neither healthy nor well.

A man came to me and said how wonderful his friend's eyes were now that he was drinking carrot juice. He said he wanted to schedule an appointment with me, at which time he said, "I think the carrot juice cure is a terrible thing. I tasted some the other day and it is awful. Have you got any cure that tastes better than carrot juice for the eyes?" When I examined his eyes, I told him that he really did need carrot juice. He wanted to know how much he had to take. I told him a quart a day. "What a terrible waste of carrot juice. You tell us we have to be happy while we're eating — how can I be happy with carrot juice going down?" I told him I didn't know, but he should do this for one month and come back to see me. At the end of the month he came back and told me what a wonderful doctor I was because his eyes were so much better since he had been drinking carrot juice. "I've even been putting that carrot juice in whiskey." I said, 'You don't really mean that you have been putting carrot juice in whiskey!!'" "Yes," he said, "Now I can see better when I'm drunk."

Do I Have To Give Up My Old Habits?

It seems people don't want to give up their old habits and ways of living — they just want to keep holding on to the old and try to add a little bit to the new.

As we become more wise we find that we have to learn to love the things we have to do. I can't talk to anyone under 50 about that. That's why everyone who comes to my lectures is over 50! I have been kidded that I don't have enough young people at my lectures. You don't find too many people who are wise when they are young. They have to get out into this mortal world that is burning, decaying and rotting to find that it is not the real thing at all.

From a physical standpoint, our physical bodies can repair twice as fast as it can break down up to the age of 30. After that, in the same amount of time, it takes twice as long to build cell structure. We must learn how to hold onto our vitality, to conserve our energy. This is the time we need wisdom more than ever. This is when we learn that the shortest distance between two points is a straight line.

The arteries don't force along the blood as fast at 50 as they do at 30. For that reason, healing is slower, but it will come if you start doing the perfect thing. At the age of 20 you only need to go half way and nature will take care of you. After 50, you have to go five-eighths of the way; after 60, you go three-quarters; after 70 you go 92%. If you are 100, you better live right if you want to go much further! You better be perfect!

When these young bodies begin to deteriorate a little bit and they find that it is futile to continue with just the physical things in life, they discover their inner need to find what is really important. This is when they start listening to my lectures on eating greens. This is when they will eat anything I say to get back their health. These are the people I can help. If they say, "Doctor, can't I just have a little piece of cake? A bottle of cola won't hurt me once in awhile will it? Do I have to quit smoking entirely? Doctor, you don't mean to take bread away from a growing girl like me do you?" What do I do with people like that?

My trouble is not my work — it's my people. Everybody else is looking for a good doctor — I'm looking for a good patient!

Speaking of young people's health . . .years ago I read that health examinations were done on the servicemen who were killed during the Korean War. It was found that 77% of those men had coronary or heart troubles. They had developed a heavy amount of cholesterol in their bodies and hardening of the arteries. This was the cream of our crop, and 77% of them had the beginning stages of coronary heart problems! Where do we start with the correction of health?

It Starts in the Kitchen

Yes, it starts in the kitchen — in the lunch box, in the school cafeterias and in our milk bottles. We must stop serving our husbands rheumatism for lunch!

I had a patient, George, who was very ill off and on with heart trouble. His wife wanted me to help him through diet and my philosophy on right living. As we sat at his bedside and started discussing some of the things he would have to do, he said, "Listen, I don't want to be told what to do. I've spent all my life telling other people what to do. I don't want to be listening to somebody else." I said, "Just how would you want to get well?" He said, "You just tell me what to do and I'll do it!" "All right, this is my word of advice: Get rid of your cook. She has cooked you into bad health and you will never get well as long as you eat her food. That's all I have to say." "Well, that's quite a blow. She has been working for us for 18 years. We don't travel anyplace unless we take her along." I said, "You aren't going to be traveling with her much longer! Is she in good health?" He said, "No — I spend almost $3,000 per year on her doctor's bills alone." I said, "You must really like her!" I said, "Well, that's all I have to say. You asked me my advice and you got it. If you want to see me again, you call me."

I didn't even get home before there was a message to go back in the morning. He said he had done a lot of thinking and decided to do some things which were against his wishes, but he gave his cook a year's salary and told her to leave. "My wife and I decided that we were going to start taking care of each other for each other's good." I was astonished at his change in consciousness. Within three months, he was buying carpeting for his new home, he started swimming in the ocean, playing 18 holes of golf per day, recovered from his heart troubles and was doing fine. There was always one thing that bothered me about him, though. Every time he came in to see me for a treatment in my Santa Monica office, he would pay me and give my nurse a $10 tip!!"

What we eat is going to walk and talk. There are no substitutes for right living. Diet can take care of 50% of the ailments; however, if I can give you any advice, it is to learn a good way of life. Do you want to raise your consciousness and live a good life? Forget about a healthy way to live. Just change your way of life — not just health more abundant, but life more abundant which includes the physical, mental and the spiritual things. We cannot just eat healthy and continue to do as we please. We must incorporate it all.

I read an article in the *San Francisco Press* which said that alcohol and crime are linked together. Over 50% of all crime comes when people are under the influence of alcohol. They go together. I wonder what goes with coffee and donuts? I am sure there is something linked with that. It is probably a level of consciousness.

It is necessary to find out how we can renew our minds so we can transform the body, think higher thoughts and attract a different type of body around us. Many overweight people have gotten that way because of emotional troubles. I know a lot of people who have broken down their glands and become wrecks due to their marriages.

I Have Even Recommended Divorce

I have even recommended divorce for health reasons. One patient in Oakland, California, had been in a mental institution for five years — two years of that she was in a straitjacket. This was the second time this had happened to her. When we helped her straighten herself out, we got the family together and I advised this young woman to get a divorce, telling her that her husband was against her and not with her — every turn she made, he refuted. I told her he was made of stone and she could not live in that home under those conditions. She did get a divorce and is very happy today, with no recurrence of her troubles. I know it is because she is happy.

You can't be well unless you are happy — really happy. I don't mean "slap happy!" Or happy like some people get wearing a $100 suit — I mean serenity and peace of mind which makes you glad you are alive and thankful that you have good friends. I mean the happiness that comes when you know you have done a good deed at the end of the day. Joy, happiness and love are three things that bathe the nervous system to such an extent that it heals all our tissues. We cannot be well unless these three things flow through us and work on our nervous systems.

All Wise Men Fasted

We know that fatigue or enervation is the beginning of every disease. We want you to stop breaking down. There are a lot of people who fast, giving up foods so they can rebuild the power within them to digest, rejuvenate and recuperate.

"Cleanse and purify thyself and I will exalt thee to the higher power." All wise men took care of their bodies — they were wise mentally, physically and spiritually. All wise men have fasted. Prior to the "Sermon on the Mount," Christ fasted for 40 days. Moses fasted for 40 days before he gave the Ten Commandments. Gandhi was a great diplomat of this world, and he fasted often to prove his points.

This is a vital thing to consider. If you don't have the power to digest your foods, what is the food going to do to you? In most cases, it will rot, spoil and produce a lot of gases and disturbances. This is why we put people on fasts — to stop. Fast means to stop all enervation — to stop all breaking down. We had a lot of people on fasts in order that they have a mental, physical and psychological rest. If you can really and truly rest, you can really do something for your body as you allow the powers to recuperate.

The salmon swim as much as 3,000 mile when they are spawning. At that time, they are also fasting. The caribou or male reindeer will fight to the finish to be the leader—the top of their herds—but they will only do it when they are fasting. If a dog breaks one of his bones, he fasts and rests completely so his body can recuperate and rebuild its tissues.

"QT" — Quiet Time

Most of us go through life a little bit faster than we should each day. We don't take time out to be quiet — we don't take time out to fast. We have Lent once a year — why shouldn't we have it more often? Why shouldn't we fast once a week? Why shouldn't we take a little meditation time out each day? If you don't like the word "meditation," why not just be quiet a little time each day? When you talk about people doing things on the "QT" — it means "quiet time." Most people think that if you do anything on the QT, it is bad or wrong. We must do something good in life. Whatever we are doing now, we are changing everything into good.

So take your next noisy moment and change it into good. Be quiet. If frustrated, make yourself quiet and serene inside. Concentrate on tranquility. Tranquility means to transfer from a state of confusion to one of quietness. If you want to transform the body, you move from the kind of body you have by renewing the mind until you transform the body. Let us transform, transfer and have the tranquility that is necessary for the body to be contented. If you cannot be contented within, you cannot get well.

13

Once again I say, the job of really getting well comes from within. This is the basis for good health. We all want good health — but we have to earn it. Christ had to dip some people seven times in the river before they got their sight back. Don't be a "doubting Thomas." "It is thy faith that has made thee whole." When one touched Christ's garment, it meant that he touched the Christ consciousness. You have to touch the consciousness of the exalted while living. As soon as you do, you are going to outpicture your sickness and take on the new. This is the divine state of which I speak.

How do we get along with people? With whom do we associate? How do we feel toward our foods? How do we feel toward our occupations and our bosses? What kind of literature do we read? What kind of music do we listen to? These all have an effect on our bodies. If we live in resentment and resistance, we eat that food and live on it. We are nourished by that type of food and will be like Swiss cheese — full of holes! We will not have a good body.

We Are What We Think

The only reason we have sickness is because we nourish it. Say to yourself "My knee is getting better and better; my knee is getting better and better; my knee is getting better and better." You will stimulate the idea and your knee will get better and better.

I have been in India where they can stop the flow going through the veins in the body and make a hair stand up on their hands. In fact, they can point to any one of their hairs and they will stand up. The power of the mind is tremendous.

I read a story about a lady and her son whose car turned over on the boy's body. The little lady, less than five feet tall, lifted the car off this boy so he could get out from under there. This is the power of thought.

Men under 150 pounds who have been put under hypnosis can lift 450 pounds. Or they can place a man with his head on one chair and feet on another chair and make his body so rigid that another person can stand on him. We can't do this under ordinary circumstances because we know our weaknesses and our strengths. But do we?

We don't know how strong we are or how powerful we are. That is why I say if we can get above this mind and mental thing, we can elevate ourselves to a higher state so we will be able to prevent anyone else from interfering with our lives. At this stage of consciousness, we could sit next to the devil and spit in his eye.

Most Of Us Start Living The Last Five Minutes Of Our Lives

We have to be strong these days because there are a lot of things in life that are so disturbing, they seem to pull on us and bring us to a state of destruction. This can affect our bodies.

Colitis, ulcers, a bad heart, high blood pressure, rectal troubles and vein troubles all start in the mind. Our minds go along with our bodies, with what we eat in life. Our minds go along with white flour and devitalized foods. Some of our minds have gone so far, they are beyond redemption. I say this very harshly because we are going to have to wake up before it's too late. Most of us start living in the last 5 minutes of our life. This is too late!

What a wonderful opportunity we have today. This is how we get our start. Remember this: God is the ruler, God is the healer, but nature is the garment around God. We can touch His garment in the green vegetables — the fresh asparagus, the ripe apricots, the bloom on the cheek of the peach.

I read that the medical doctor who was the head of the American Neurological Society said that twenty percent of the men in this country were sterile — unable to produce children. He claimed that it was due to the fact that they don't have the right foods, and vitamin E was lacking in their cooked foods. White flour is void of vitamin E. However, there is vitamin E in the rice polishings of brown rice. When the whole wheat berry is refined, the vitamin E is gone. Anti-sterility vitamins are then wiped away.

These facts are startling! One-fifth of the men in this country are sterile due to a lack of vitamin E! Seventy-seven percent of our men who died in Korea had coronary disease! One in ten people are well in our country at the age of forty. Ninety-two percent of the people are sick in this country! You can see we are trying to make a living when we are not well! We are trying to be happy with poor physical bodies. It is time we put the physical and the mental together. There is a lot of work for us to do.

PRESS ON

NOTHING IN THE WORLD CAN TAKE THE PLACE OF PERSISTENCE. TALENT WILL NOT; NOTHING IS MORE COMMON THAN UNSUCCESSFUL MEN WITH TALENT. GENIUS WILL NOT; UNREWARDED GENIUS IS ALMOST A PROVERB. EDUCATION ALONE WILL NOT; THE WORLD IS FULL OF EDUCATED DERELICTS. PERSISTENCE AND DETERMINATION ALONE ARE OMNIPOTENT.

President CALVIN A. COOLIDGE

16

CHAPTER 1

THE CHEMICAL STORY

We need specific chemicals in order to produce good bodies. I speak briefly of them here, and suggest you delve more deeply into them in my book, **The Chemistry of Man**.

We need sodium to keep young — sodium is the youth element which gives us softness and tenderness in the tissues. Sodium keeps calcium from settling in the body and producing arthritis. Sodium is found highest in goat milk, okra, celery, soybean milk and especially whey, which is the drippings from cheese after milk has been curdled. Many people believe that cheese is binding and constipating. It is binding because the whey is separated from the cheese when it is curdled — we eat what is left over. The whey is the laxative part of the milk. Whey, being very high in sodium, is what we need to keep our joints limber, active and pliable. So, if you are going to have cheese, have a little whey along with it. Drink a glass of whey — it will make your cheese complete again.

I picked up some bones in Spokane, Washington, from horses where ranchers were having trouble with horses' bones growing together. It was found that there was a lack of sodium — the youth element — in the bones. There was a lack of salt to complete the body metabolism. Ankylosis is not uncommon. When your bones begin to get stiff and hard, the doctor tells you that you are getting old. Actually, you are simply lacking the chemical sodium which is keeping your joints limber and pliable.

Sodium is a bowel element. To have good bowel movements, we must have sodium, as it balances the intestinal flora and keeps it in the proper acid/alkaline balance. We have friendly bacteria we must keep active in the bowel, and sodium is the element needed to feed the bowel to keep this friendly bacteria alive. Many people are using acidophilus culture and acidophilus milk for their bowels. Always have sodium with acidophilus. I don't mean sodium as in table salt. Sodium foods help us get rid of gases in the bowel.

We highly respect the work of John Harvey Kellogg who discovered that death began in the bowel. Life begins in the bowel. Deterioration in our body begins in the bowel. Catarrhal conditions, sinus trouble, bronchitis, asthma, etc., all begin in and have to be taken care of first through the bowel. When the bowel becomes clean, the breath becomes sweet, the tongue becomes clean, the tartar on our teeth lessens. We have to have a clean bowel.

Sir Lane, the King of England's physician, took care of the bowel. His specialty was to remove sections of the bowel which had become emaciated and broken down — he taught other doctors how to repair specific parts of the bowel, depending on the affliction. In one case, a lady had a huge goiter, and after his bowel operation, it reduced itself within six months to become normal. A young boy had arthritis and was bound to a wheelchair for fourteen years. Sir Lane removed a section of this boy's bowel which was ballooned and toxic, and the boy was out of the wheelchair and walking, without arthritis, within six months.

Sir Lane then turned to diet consultation with his patients, noting the improved conditions of the bowel through X-rays. In the last ten years of his life, he gave up operations entirely and counseled solely on diets which were pure, whole and natural.

Silicon, Calcium, Magnesium And Iron

Silicon gives us the magnetic qualities in our bodies. We don't have proper coordination between the mind and the muscle structure without the proper silicon in the body. A rash on the body shows a lack of silicon. When our hair gets dry, we lack silicon. Boils and discharges from the body indicate a lack of silicon. Oatstraw and shavegrass tea are very high in silicon.

When we do not have the power to repair and rebuild, we don't have enough calcium in the body. When we cannot knit bones or tissues, we need calcium.

Magnesium gives us the tone and balances the alkaline conditions in the bowel. Magnesium is found in yellow corn meal — it is one of the highest foods in magnesium as well as phosphates...(4%).

18

You might be interested to know that white corn meal has two percent phosphates. Phosphates are needed to feed the brain and the nervous system as well as sulphur, iodine, phosphorus and manganese.

If we have a temper tantrum, we show a lack of iodine. If we can't stand going up in an elevator, we lack iodine. If we can't stand anything tight around our neck, we lack iodine. Clam juice is high in iodine, as well as nettle tea.

Oxygen is held in the body by iron. Without the proper amount of iron in the body, we don't have enough oxygen. If you want to have more oxygen to burn up the waste in your body or to assimilate the food which goes into the body, you need more iron. Iron foods are cherry juice (one of the best) and blackberries (although constipating). Green foods are iron building — they attract oxygen from the air we breathe.

Fluorine is also needed in the body in order to get enough oxygen. Fluorine is the anti-resistance element and is only found in raw foods. Cooked foods no longer have fluorine in them. There is 10 times as much fluorine in goat's milk as in cow's milk, both of which are the highest foods we have in fluorine. Pasteurized milk does not give you enough fluorine to keep you well.

Herbs For The Body

When we get close to nature, our whole body is taken care of. If we want to learn a little bit about herbs, find out what papaya-mint tea will do for the stomach. Every one of us should know what alfalfa-mint tea will do. Mint is a great cleanser for the stomach. Do we want to sweeten up the intestinal tract? Get a little sassafras tea. Chamomile tea is a wonderful builder for the intestinal tract. If we have any disturbances with the intestinal tract, such as inflammation, find out what flaxseed tea will do. Find out what peach-leaf tea can do for you. Elderberry blossom tea is excellent for the kidneys. Elderberries are the finest ovarian tonic, for menstrual cramps and monthly disorders. Violet tea is good for heavy catarrhal conditions, as it drains the lymph glands and heavy mucus. Violet tea is good for bronchitis and asthma. Nature is so bountiful in what she can do for you — all you have to do is go out and be part of it.

19

Get down and touch some of the herbs. Huckleberry tea is the most wonderful thing for diabetes. We have a little stout lady who visits us, and she is so happy because she got rid of 5 inches around her waist. But you don't hear her say under her breath that she got rid of diabetes also. How is it that she can get rid of two things at the same time?

The Cure Is Not In A Bottle

We think cure is in a box, an office, and we think we have to pay for it in a certain bottle. It is a mystery and a wonder for which we all search, and it is right out in the sunshine, the air and up in the hills. People have come from Sweden and Norway to visit Salt Lake City and their whole bodies became upset because they cannot take the altitude. For years, they lived at sea level. In just a matter of a short time — flying to this country — they arrived in Salt Lake City and found they didn't feel right. When they went back to the ocean, they felt good again. Climate surely has much to do with our activities and our feelings in life.

Go To The Mountains For A High Blood Count

Here is a lesson from those who live in Peru in the Andes. Some of them live in 10-12,000 foot altitudes. They have a blood count that is 7,500,000. The highest blood count you can get at the ocean is 5,000,000. So if you have to rebuild your blood, go to the hills — the higher you go, the higher your blood count becomes and the more ozone there is in the air.

Learn about skin brushing. More people with bronchial troubles, bronchitis and catarrhal discharges in the body alleviate their symptoms when they start skin brushing.

What does it take to become healthy? Is it just the diet? No, it is the combination of skin brushing, the slant board, the diet and/or climate — plus our positive attitude. What does it? It is living on the whole garment of God, which is all of nature.

Touch The Greens!

Touch the greens — they will make you clean inside. When you are green inside, you are clean inside. Chlorophyll from plant life is indispensable for good health. One cancer specialist used green juices constantly for his cancer patients. Green is high in potassium, which is the muscular element — the heart element. Potassium is the alkalizer in the body. It is called the healer in the body. Who doesn't want a healing? Who is going to give you your healing? Get it in the greens — get it in juices — get it in your foods and your diet. That is where the healing is. Don't expect a healer to pass his hand over you and say you are well. It doesn't work that way.

Another thing I must tell you is that you cannot expect to get well in less than a year. No. It takes a year to make good tissue and it takes time!

All That Touches The Body Goes Into The Body

And of course, our thinking is very important. The mind is very powerful. One lady received word from the government that her husband had been killed in Korea. She was nursing her baby at the time, and in less than five minutes, the baby died. Why? The shock material and the emotional acids produced by this mother actually killed her baby. What a shock!

It has been found that a nursing mother produces nicotine in her milk in less than two minutes after she starts puffing on a cigarette. That's how fast we absorb what we take into our bodies.

While at the Battle Creek Sanitarium, a man soaked his feet in baking soda water. In less than thirty seconds, a urine sample from him was tested and baking soda was found in his urine.

Can we afford to put anything in our body but the best, knowing that it is going to go to the kidneys, the stomach, the eye structure and various parts of our body? The same thing happens with drugs. Food goes into the body to rebuild, reconstruct, develop and rejuvenate. Drugs break down and destruct the body tissues. Drugs do not have a constructive effect in the body. This is why we turn you back to nature and the use of natural, pure and whole foods.

The Value Of An Elimination Diet

If you are truly interested in working out your problems, the first thing I recommend is to find out the value of an elimination diet. Know the limits of an elimination diet. Immediately following an elimination diet, the first thing you need to do is find a healthy way to live.

A healthy way to live is a mental, physical and spiritual thing. Mother taught me years ago what a good life is — a good mental life and a good spiritual life. Just let that flow through you. Don't ever try to make life happen. I can see so many people trying to make life happen. "I'll do this if it kills me," they say, "I'll get there at 8 o'clock if I have to crawl." That's what I do and say in my life. I am sure you have your own pressures which are destroying you as well.

Your body will automatically get well if you give it a good environment, because it is self-rejuvenating and self-recuperating. Most of us cheat ourselves out of many things in life. While you are striving to get well, don't always think about the things you have committed, think sometimes of the things you have omitted.

Come Up For Air!

Fasting and juice dieting are all right — but get on with it and learn a healthy way to live. The healthy way to live starts at the table, with most people. While we can't live very long without food, we can't live as long without water and still less time without air. They are signing death certificates all the time for babies born with pneumonia, bronchial troubles — and they died from the effects of smog! We have to go where there is fresh air. Come up for air!

Sunshine is wonderful also. There are two places on your body that should have sunshine — the long bones of the body and the spine. We don't need to worry about the rest of the body. You can have a sunbath right in front of your open window. You don't always have to be outside. The average window glass filters about ninety-eight percent of the ultraviolet light. Ultraviolet light is what is necessary to control the calcium in the body.

Calcium is the chemical element that gives us tone, energy and power with which to work. Calcium is the healing element in the body — the knitter. Whenever we have to knit any condition in our bodies whether it be ulcers, bones or tissues, we need calcium. It is one of the first chemical elements we should use. Sunshine controls calcium in the body. You can't live without calcium, and you can't live without sunshine. They go together. That is why we take cod liver oil — the vitamin B - in the winter, because we don't get enough sunshine. In the summer, we don't take cod liver oil because we get plenty of sunshine.

They claim that in ten minutes of sunshine, you can get enough vitamin B to last you for three days. So you don't need any long sunbathing. Don't go to the beach and lie there until you come back like crisp bacon — this breaks down the body. Take your sunshine a little bit every day.

Artificial Sunlight

Some have asked about artificial sunlight or sunlamps. I think they are fine for those who don't have sunshine. A Danish scientist discovered that sunlight has an effect on the bloodstream of the body. He found that the sunlamp helped to also build the red blood cells in the body, so he made a copy of the sunshine, called a mercury arc lamp or sunlight bulbs. There are many tanning salons popular now where you can get a tan with artificial sunlight. But, it is artificial — it is a substitute. I don't think it is as good as the real thing. For that reason, I feel you should try to get natural sunshine when you can. On the other hand, if you can't get the best food, you take the next best. The same is true with the ultraviolet light. However, always remember, substitutes will let you down quicker than a strapless gown!

Eyeglasses And Ultraviolet

Another little secret I have learned is that sunglasses cut out about ninety-eight percent of the ultraviolet control of calcium in the body. I suggest that people who wear glasses remove their glasses three to four hours a day when outside. It is not meant that they should get sunlight directly in their eyes, but the light or reflection will do an enormous amount of good. If I wore glasses, there would be only one glass I would use — the new Corning glass. It allows ninety-eight percent of the ultraviolet light in, rather than keep it out as average glass products.

I learned this from John Opp who wrote **The Ivory Cellar**. At his home in Chicago, he shared his findings which he discovered while working with Walt Disney developing time lapse photography. He discovered that an apple blossom would mature and blossom for about four days under natural light. But when the light was put through his glasses to the apple blossom, it would only come out half to three-quarters of a day and would not develop anymore.

Fluorescent Lights And Vitamin A

Fluorescent lights are injurious to our health — they rob the body of vitamin A. Vitamin A helps rid the body of germ life. Catarrhal problems and colds indicate we are lacking vitamin A. Deafness is a result of a lack of vitamin A, as are polyps, nasal disturbances and sinus disturbances. Fluorescent lights contribute to this problem. I don't think we will ever find all the things that disturb, destroy and kill us in our lives, but we should be aware that there is a negative and a positive, darkness and light, right and wrong, good and bad. We should be aware of the fact that we should strive for the **best** in life — which will always be found in nature. We are children of nature. We are not children of the apartment house, the freeway or of frustration. We are children of God — good and natural. We should be the children of love and live so that God is in our midst. We should live so that whatever we do, we have the approval of heaven. We cannot do the wrong thing and expect the right thing to happen. If we do the right thing, right will right itself.

Some Extra Health Tips

Cream is probably the most natural of all fats to go into the body. Cream can be taken into the body with the least amount of trouble. There are some people who cannot take it and some people should not take it. Raw cream (not pasteurized), whipped cream and sour cream are good used in our salad dressings in place of the many oils which we are presently using.

I believe we are going overboard on oils in our diets. We should never use heated oil, which will disturb the body and produce cholesterol.

Use raw milk whenever you can. Learn how to make soy milk and soy cream. Soy milk with safflower oil and vanilla can be whipped into a healthy whipped cream.

Always have vegetables with your sandwiches. Never eat bread and cheese without vegetables. Vegetables hold the water, while starches dry out and cause constipation.

My first recommendation to all people is to cut out bread if you possible can — even good bread. I do serve bread at my ranch when we have classes and visitors. I go halfway with you at first, just like the preacher who traveled to church where he was scheduled to preach. When he reached the pulpit, he found only one man in the congregation. He looked at this man and said, "It is hard to believe I came all the way out here to give a sermon and you are the only one here. Do you think I ought to give the sermon?" The man replied, "When my sheep come in and they are hungry, I feed them." The preacher went on to give his sermon and when he was finished, two hours later, he asked the lone man in the congregation, "Did you like that sermon?" The man looked up and said, "When my sheep are hungry, I feed them, but I don't give them the whole load the first time!"

So we start slowly with you at first when we discuss a healthy way to live — we don't want to give you the whole load the first time.

If you want to join us, there is more to learn and you can be more and more strict as you get into it. I want you to learn to take care of yourself. Doctors make a living on your living. It is about time you begin to live a different way.

Learn what exercise is — don't ever expect diet alone to get you well, you need exercise, good foods, good thinking, good companionship, a good attitude while you're eating, and learning from every experience that comes into your life. Turn around and be thankful for that which is yet to come.

Bless people instead of condemning them. Love your enemy because he is the only one who tells you your faults. You have to love for your own good. Your enemy and your neighbor do not need your love — you do.

As we combine it all, recognize that you are on your own.

We are what we think and we can go through life a pauper or we can go through life richly blessed:

I asked God for strength that I might achieve,
But I was made weak that I might learn humbly to obey.

I asked for health that I might do greater things,
But I was given infirmity that I might do better things.

I asked for riches that I might be happy,
I was given poverty that I might be wise.

I asked for power that I might have the praise of men,
I was given weakness that I might feel the need of God.

I asked for all things that I might enjoy life,
But I was given life that I might enjoy all things.

I got nothing that I asked for, but everything I hoped for.
Almost despite myself, my unspoken prayers were answered.
I am among men, most richly blessed.

CHAPTER 2

CATARRH AS A HOST FOR DISEASE

Catarrh is the universal symptom of imbalances in the body, indicating disease-producing processes at work. It is always the first symptom to appear and it always indicates an excess of acids and mucus being developed due to tissue inflammation. Catarrh can be caused by a deficiency of the biochemical elements, an imbalance or excess of them or a toxic irritant in the body.

Catarrh is derived from the Greek words *cata* (down) and *rhein* (flow) — to flow down. It is the body's normal response to tissue inflammation and as long as catarrh is allowed to flow, we know the body's natural defense system is working properly. Its presence often signals the onset of a cold, flu or other elimination process, but the most universal response to it is to run to the doctor or drugstore and get a drug to stop it.

We find that catarrh is not so much a cause of disease as a sign that something is wrong in the body. That is, it is part of the body's natural response to some other condition. Yet, when we suppress catarrh, when we drive it back into the body, we force it to collect in some organ or tissue where it becomes a host for germ life and viruses. Everything in the body must move to accomplish its function, and catarrh is no exception. When we stop the flow of catarrh by using drugs, we are planting the seeds of chronic disease.

Every "itis" — tonsillitis, bronchitis, sinusitis, appendicitis and all the others — are fundamentally inflammation diseases accompanied by catarrh. Healing cannot take place unless the catarrh formed to carry off toxic material is eliminated from the body. Then the inflammation will be taken care of by the body's natural immune system. Suppression of catarrh with drugs is not true healing, but only the temporary elimination of symptoms.

Catarrh

Diptheria is a catarrhal disorder, characterized by development of a coating in the membrane of the throat that gives off a foul mucus.

Consumption is an advanced stage of chronic catarrh of the lungs, resulting from years of feeding on faulty foods.

Catarrh often affects the Eustachian tube, leading from the throat to the tympanic membrane, or ear drum, causing deafness. It may result in suppurlative inflammation or an abcess may form if not taken care of.

In women, the catarrhal condition may extend to the mucus membrane of the vagina, passing up into the uterus and out the Fallopian tubes, where the effect is in severe, delayed, painful or protracted menstruation. The ovaries may become involved, and the disorder is often treated with unnecessary surgery.

In both sexes, the catarrhal inflammation often extends to the kidneys and on to the bladder, causing bladder stones and other disorders of the genitourinary system.

In fact, when the body becomes well saturated with the acid poisons resulting from poor food habits, a person will suffer from one or more of many catarrhal disorders named as follows:

- Catarrh of the stomach, called gastritis.
- Catarrh of the mouth, called stomatitis.
- Catarrh of the throat, called diphtheritis (diphtheria).
- Catarrh of the nose, called rhinitis.
- Catarrh of the bronchi, called bronchitis (hay fever, asthma, etc.).
- Catarrh of the lungs, called pulmonitis (influenza, pneumonia, consumption).

- Catarrh of the eyes, called conjuctivitis (trachoma).
- Catarrh of the ears, called otitis.
- Catarrh of the brain, called meningitis.
- Catarrh of the small intestine, called enteritis.
- Catarrh of the large intestine, called colitis.
- Catarrh of the appendix, called appendicitis.
- Catarrh of the liver, called hepatitis.
- Catarrh of the pancreas, called pancreatitis.
- Catarrh of the kidneys, called nephritis (Bright's disease).
- Catarrh of the vagina, called vaginitis (leucorrhea).
- Catarrh of the uterus, called metritis.
- Catarrh of the ovaries, called ovaritis.
- Catarrh of the prostate, called prostatitis.
- Catarrh of the joints, called arthritis.
- Catarrh of the veins, called phlebitis.
- Catarrh of the arteries, called arteritis.
- Catarrh of the heart, called carditis, pericarditis, endocarditis, etc.

The above list, while far from complete, serves well to show two things: (1) how medical institutions name immaterial symptoms, according to their location, and foolishly treat each symptom as a different disease, while disregarding the cause responsible for the symptoms, thus leaving the cause to continue its degenerative work; and (2) how one harmful habit, although apparently insignificant, when steadily pursued deranges the whole body, establishing slowly but surely a chronic condition that finally affects every organ, structure and function.

As the body normally functions, mucus is made by goblet cells in the mucus membranes lining the alimentary system, the respiratory system and parts of the genitourinary system. This mucus lubricates and protests the sensitive tissue lining these parts of the anatomy. If germ life, foreign matter or toxic substances enter the body, they are entrapped in the sticky mucus which is eventually excreted from the body as catarrh — flowing mucus.

Cystic fibrosis is an inherited glandular disorder caused by a defective gene which results in excessive salty perspiration and thick mucus secretion instead of the normal thin mucus. Lung and digestive problems are consequences. The thick mucus can plug the small pancreas ducts, stopping the flow of its digestive juices and hindering digestion. Symptoms often include very salty perspiration, coughing, wheezing, lung infections, big appetitie with no weight gain and bulky, foul-smelling stools.

Catarrhal Conditions

Junk food diets are among the most common causes of catarrh. There is so much material in junk food that the body can't digest or assimilate that it must be eliminated as waste. Diets high in certain starches and proteins can produce catarrh. Over 50% of the average American diet consists of wheat and milk products, and any allergy specialist can testify that these are heavy catarrh producers in many people. On a recent visit to China, I noticed people spitting everywhere, probably due to a concentration of white rice in the diet. By and large, Oriental people avoid the more nutritious brown rice, calling it "dirty rice." I believe many of them would rather starve than eat brown rice, but the price they pay for their heavy white rice diet is catarrh.

Breathing polluted air can cause catarrhal conditions in the lungs. Any external irritant taken into the body will produce catarrh.

I have found some persons who produce catarrh much more easily than others, no doubt due to a sensitive metabolism or perhaps a lack of certain enzymes. In fact, it is possible for the body to load up with acidic wastes and catarrh simply because of one or more underactive elimination channels.

Normally, the body is busily replacing old cells with new ones, and metabolic wastes are carried away at roughly the same rate that new nutrients and building materials come in. But, whenever one of the elimination channels is underactive — bowels, kidneys, lungs, skin or lymphatic system — the others must try to pick up the overload or else catarrh builds up in the body. The bowel is the most frequent problem, but any of the elimination systems can be involved. Without sufficient exercise, the lymph doesn't move fast enough, and accumulations of waste and toxic materials can build up at the lymph nodes in the groin, under the arms, in the neck and elsewhere. Kidney problems are not uncommon, particularly

30

since they so often develop as side affects from conditions like atherosclerosis and diabetes. It is possible for the cholesterol to block the fine blood capillaries under the skin, reducing the elimination via the skin. There are many ways in which the efficiency of the eliminative organs can be reduced. Smoking and polluted air, of course, hinder the lungs from expelling toxins and catarrh. If any of the elimination systems are slowed down, catarrhal buildup in the body can be due to metabolic wastes alone, even if the diet is basically good.

Genetic factors may contribute to catarrhal conditions. Everyone is born with certain strengths and weaknesses in the body, but the strengths don't create problems so we only have to take care of the weaknesses. When the digestion or assimilation are weak, more catarrh is produced. When any of the eliminative organs is under-active, more catarrh is produced. When certain enzymes are lacking or when the thyroid is underactive, more catarrh is produced. Chill or fatigue affect the weaker organs and tissues more severely than other parts of the body, allowing catarrh to develop.

In my experience, one of the most common causes of catarrh production is fatigue. A tired body is not eliminating well, and it develops acids that are not quickly removed from the body.

We find that catarrh does not become a problem in the body as long as we keep it moving. In terms of physiology, the life of the body is in the constant movement of the thousands of processes that keep everything going. Movement is life; stasis is death. When anything slows down in the body, irritation develops and catarrh is produced. If catarrh itself slows down or stops, it irritates tissue and promotes more catarrh. We find also that slowing down any process in the body always affects the other processes dependent on it. Eventually, everything in the body is affected to some degree, by a single change. If nutrients are stopped, cells starve, die and begin to decompose almost immediately, resulting in more catarrh. Of course, bacteria and germ life thrive on dead matter, and more catarrh is produced as the body's natural immune system goes to work against them.

It would be safe to say that there are a thousand and one causes of catarrh. But there is one fundamental and appropriate response to catarrh: let it run — or better yet, help the body get rid of it faster.

VALUES OF LIFE

Supposing today were your last on earth;
The last mile of the journey you've trod;
After all your struggles how much are you worth?
How much can you take home to God?

Don't count as possessions your silver or gold;
For tomorrow you leave them behind;
And all that is yours to have and to hold,
Are the blessings you've given mankind.

Just what have you done as you journeyed along;
That was really and truly worthwhile?
Do you think your good deeds would offset the wrong?
Could you look o'er your life with a smile?

We are only supposing, but if it were real,
And you invoiced your deeds since your birth;
And you figured the "profits" you've made in life's deal;
How much are you really worth?

— Anonymous

Consequence of Suppression

Over the past few decades, the elimination of the common cold and other catarrhal conditions have almost become a crusade with drug manufacturers. Drug companies compete with their TV ads over which drug gives the fastest, most effective "relief" of symptoms. By relief they mean suppression.

The common cold is regarded as a viral disease by Western medicine, but doctors cannot account for why some people are so susceptible to colds while others never get them at all. It apparently doesn't occur to them that diet, constitutional strength and inherent weaknesses determine the degree of tissue response to any irritant — and whether or not inflammation and catarrh will develop. A virus does not "cause" anything. We are constantly exposed to viruses and bacteria of many dangerous types, yet we seldom are affected by them unless our bodies become depleted by nutrient deficiency and tissue becomes inflamed. Germ life must have substance to feed on or it cannot thrive and reproduce. and O_2

According to experts, the viruses differ greatly among individuals with colds, which is why a vaccine can't be developed for the common cold. As we grow older, our immunity to colds appears to increase. We should not take suppressant drugs for cold symptoms but let the catarrh which develops flow out of the body.

To suppress catarrh requires driving it back into the tissues of the body, along with all the germ life, foreign matter and toxic accumulations it contains. There it functions as a low-grade poison, interfering with tissue metabolism and serving as a continuing irritant. The usual consequence is the development of chronic disease, the type of disease depending on the inherent weaknesses of the individual.

Most Americans fail to realize the price they pay for suppressing catarrh. A cough, for example, is a natural reflex action to rid the upper bronchials of catarrh. From the advertisements of some cough medicines, we find they work by suppressing the cough center in the medulla of the brain, where there are also centers relating to the heart, lungs and digestion. How can a drug affect the cough center without affecting the other vital centers in the same brain area? Other drugs act to dry up catarrh in the body, inviting the development of abnormal tissue pathology wherever the dried catarrh settles.

We find that the first operation most people have is a tonsillectomy. The tonsils are lymph tissue, and tonsillitis is an inflammation of the lymph tissue due to toxic overload. To remove the tonsils is like trying to solve a garbage problem by getting rid of the garbage trucks, and it doesn't work. After the tonsils, the next operation is often an appendectomy, and the appendix is also lymph tissue. Each time lymph tissue is removed, the body has to find some other place to send catarrh and lymphatic waste. So, we encounter fibroid tumors and cysts in the breast tissue (also lymphatic), or in the lungs, stomach, bowel or pelvic area. The catarrh **must** go somewhere when it is suppressed, and it always causes problems when it is not allowed to flow out of the body.

Suppression of catarrh is always an invitation to disease.

The Four Stages of Disease

All diseases go through four stages — acute, subacute, chronic and degenerative. The acute stage is the active stage of disease, usually accompanied by catarrh, fever, coughing, inflammation and soreness localized in the body. Catarrh may issue from any orifice in the body, and strands of it may be found in the urine. In the acute stage, the body is actively trying to throw off the disease, and all organs are hyperactive to support the elimination.

The subacute stage is more serious. If the body fails to throw off the disease in the acute, running stage, the inflammation sinks deeper into the tissues, reducing the metabolic rate and further weakening the body. The chronic stage finds the body in a lower condition yet. This is where flu, colds and hay fever turn into asthma, with occasional bouts of pneumonia. This is where joint aches turn into chronic arthritis. The final or degenerative stage is very nearly the point of no return. Asthma turns to emphysema. The joints swell and grow, calcium spurs appear, in the arthritis case. Lumps and tumors are found to be malignant.

Most poor health in adults can be traced back to childhood conditions. All children's problems such as colds, flu, earaches, mumps, measles and tonsillitis should be taken care of by natural means to prevent catarrh from being driven back into the body. Cleanliness, correct foods, stimulating activities and pleasant surroundings with plenty of love will keep most children well. Herbal and other natural supplements may be needed from time to time, but suppressants must be avoided.

Nature's way is to let catarrh run until the source of irritation and inflammation is throw off.

Iridology and Catarrh

In iridology, we examine the iris and find out where catarrhal congestion is in the body. We can look at the bowel area and see if it is underactive. We can examine the kidneys for acute or subacute conditions. If the skin is underactive, we will find a scurf rim around the edge of the iris, and if the lungs and bronchials are underactive, they will show up darker than other areas. Lymphatic congestion may be demonstrated by the appearance of puffy white or yellowish dots around the inner circumference of the iris, sometimes called "lymphatic rosary" or "string of pearls."

Underactive elimination organs are one indication of catarrhal problems, but there is another obvious sign. Any eye which is acute and white, with many iris fibers raised above the surface, is considered an acidic eye, representing heavy catarrhal conditions in the body. An acid eye is a sign that the body is, almost literally, a catarrh factory.

We can tell, with the help of iridology, which organs and tissues of the body are deficient in nutrients or are toxic laden. Either can be a basic cause of catarrh. Iridology, in fact, tells us exactly what we need to know to correct the physical side of the problem.

Elimination of Catarrh

When iridology discloses biochemical deficiencies in various organs, we can make diet and nutrition basic considerations in our approach to eliminating catarrh. There are two basic steps in getting rid of catarrh, and they both work together. Cleansing the body through fasting, juices and bowel management is half of the solution. Correct nutrition is the other half. We purify the body as much as we can and we strengthen it as much as we can. This assumes that we are changing food and other habits which contribute to or aggravate the catarrhal problem, because our goal is to strengthen the body until it can throw off toxic accumulations through the reversal process and the healing crisis.

Hering's law of cure says, "All cure starts from the head down, from the inside out and in reverse order as symptoms have first appeared." Each time we have built the body up through right nutrition, exercise, recreation and rest to the place where it reaches a certain level of strength, a healing crisis occurs in which old symptoms of disease are retraced and catarrh is liquified and thrown off. Depending on how chronic or degenerative the disease has become, it may take several healing crises to eliminate the old catarrhal deposits.

Here, iridology is a wonderful tool. Not only can we identify which parts of the body are toxic laden and which are deficient, we can tell when a healing crisis is approaching and when healing is taking place in the tissues. In other words, we can monitor our progress with each patient. Often we find that patients going through a healing crisis can taste the suppressive drugs and medications they have taken in the past — quinine, coal tar drugs and sulphur-based medications to name a few.

I have never had a person under my care for a year or more who did not notice better bowel function, fewer colds and higher well-being than in many years. Any who have experienced catarrhal discharges from any part of their body notice definite improvement. Properly selected foods made a decisive difference in ridding the body of catarrh.

Lord Chichester, after discovering he had cancer, went on a grape diet and sailed around the world. By the end of his trip, the cancer had disappeared. Asthma can be taken care of if we get rid of the miasmic background present in asthmatics. Some of this may even have been inherited from their parents. Likewise, to get rid of colitis, an inflammation of the large bowel, we must get rid of the mucus strings in the colon. Much of the process of healing, no matter what the disease, requires elimination of catarrh from the body.

This is it

36

An Ounce of Prevention

It is time we realized that there is a way of living which will bring the cell structure of the body to the highest possible integrity. The great majority of people walk around living between a subacute and chronic condition, unable to do their work competently, be on time, think efficiently, remember well or enjoy their energy, and their state of well-being is flying at half-mast. It is all so unnecessary.

When we eat right, exercise properly, get enough sunshine, fresh air and rest, think positively and live so that we can lift others into a better way of life, our own lives reach the state of high-level well-being that makes it a joy to be alive.

CHAPTER 3

FATIGUE

Although I have said that catarrh precedes the development of every disease, there is another symptom that precedes catarrh and is extremely dangerous on its own account. The following news article appeared in the Escondido *Times-Advocate* on February 2, 1983:

Fatigue cited in part for crash

SAN JOSE — Pilot fatigue may have played a part in the collision of a light plane and a PSA jetliner over San Diego that killed 144 people, according to two researchers.

"Interrupted sleep patterns and no sleep for 15 hours may have contributed to the crash," said Daniel C. Holley and William Price, of San Jose State University. They are investigating the role of sleep loss in three crashes, including one in San Diego in 1978.

"The collision came nine seconds after the small plane was finally sighted," Prince said. "With total rest and in the best of circumstances, it takes six seconds to sight danger, analyze it and take action."

Fatigue is the signal that is meant to tell us, like a blinking red light or a siren, that the danger point has been reached in the body's energy level. Reaction time is slower, as are all mental functions. The rational mind doesn't function as well. Digestion and assimilation are poor. All body systems are affected by fatigue.

We find that many accidents are caused by fatigue. When a person is tired, fatigued and mentally sluggish, his attention span is lessened. His physical capability and activity level are lowered. His personality changes and his nerve and heart activity dwindle. His temper becomes short, and his temperament evidences such changes as grouchiness, depression, pessimism, antagonism, irrational anger, cruelty, coldness, poor judgment, indecisiveness and confusion. The shift in mental states plus the slowed reaction time makes accidents much more likely. Notice in the plane crash article, the two researchers stated that six seconds would normally have been sufficient for a rested pilot to observe danger and take evasive action. The crash occurred nine seconds after the smaller plane was sighted, which led the researchers to believe that fatigue was an important component.

Common Fatigue Procedures

What produces fatigue? There are many factors. One is the operation of reticular activating system in the brain stem, which strongly influences our sleep/wake cycles, probably in conjunction with the hypothalamus. We cannot go without sleep for too long, even if we eat well, since the brain and body need rest to rejuvenate and repair cells and to eliminate metabolic wastes. Another factor is the lowering of blood sugar. The brain uses something like 20% of the blood glucose to energize its activities, and when the blood glucose level falls, brain efficiency is reduced, and a feeling of fatigue is experienced. Still other factors are the amount of oxygen in the blood, the buildup of acid wastes in the body, the depletion of hormone levels and reduction of nerve efficiency. It may well be that the available levels of neurotransmitters such as acetylcholine influence fatigue.

Different Sources of Fatigue

Fatigue, interestingly enough, can be produced in many ways. Lack of sleep, hard physical labor, mental work, monotony, anxiety, emotional extremes, stress, starvation (or malnutrition) and various psychological problems can produce or bring on fatigue.

People often feel tired after having arguments, or simply spending time with someone they don't like. Driving a car or any other vehicle, especially on a busy freeway, can be fatiguing. A sustained period of intense concentration, as required during driving in heavy traffic or taking a test, may be the primary cause. Often, under such conditions, the neck and back muscles tense up, using extra energy and speeding up the onset of fatigue. Once I had to drive through heavy freeway traffic four hours to get to an appointment on time. When I arrived, I found that I almost had to pry my fingers loose from the steering wheel. Any physiological or mental process done under stress is fatigue-producing.

Fear is followed by fatigue, after the adrenalin hormone wears off. Joy, surprise, excitement — extremes of either positive or negative emotion — take their toll of energy and contribute to tiredness. Excessive sexual indulgence can create fatigue. Consuming large quantities of alcohol may put the brain in a stupor, but it also takes a great deal of energy to detoxify the body via the liver.

Heavy drinkers often feel tired, fatigued.

Some sources of fatigue may be traced to brain centers such as the Animation and Life Center, as we call it in iridology. Some years ago, Dr. J. Haskel Kritzer, one of the pioneer iridologists in the United States, called this part of the iris the "Fatigue Center," but I changed it to Animation and Life Center because its normal function is more accurately conveyed by that term. Fatigue is simply one of its low-level functions when this center is out of balance.

Fatigue due to physical or stress-related causes is often followed by psychological expressions of it; psychological expressions of this syndrome are often followed by physical fatigue, tiredness, loss of energy and vitality. This appears to be a two-way interrelationship here.

Stages of Fatigue

For some persons at least, fatigue has several stages. The initial stage is tiredness, but if a person works past that period, a kind of lightheadedness or giddiness develops. This is sometimes accompanied by extreme talkativeness or its opposite, silence. The next stage is a type of dull stupor. The work continues at a slower pace as the body endures, performing more on nerve energy and perhaps on fat reserves than anything else. Lapses of memory may occur. A speaker may pause in mid-sentence, having completely forgotten what he or she was saying. A worker may lay a tool down in the vicinity of his work, then, needing it again, may spend fifteen minutes looking for it. Work goes slower and slower as the body and mind approach total exhaustion.

The advanced stages of fatigue are extremely dangerous for anyone using tools or machinery with moving parts. It is often at this stage that automobile drivers "fall asleep at the wheel" and drive off the road. Sawmill workers cut off fingers in saws or get arms crushed by moving logs. Carpenters fall off scaffolds. People drop things, hit their heads on cupboard doors and slip in bathtubs when they are extremely fatigued.

Fatigue at this stage can throw off the reticular activating system and disrupt the normal sleep/wake cycle. An extremely fatigued person may go to bed then toss and turn uncomfortably, unable to sleep. It is almost as though fatigue produces, in some, a sleep-inhibiting chemical.

At the other end of the scale, body builders use short-term muscle fatigue as a means of building larger muscles. "Pumping iron," as the body builders call it, is a systematic workout in which different muscle groups are "stress fatigued" by repetitions of weight lifting or moving. Blood rushes to each area exercised, bringing oxygen and nutrients, carrying off wastes.. Properly done, body building includes correct eating habits and plenty of rest at night.

Most forms of exercise work on this principle. Temporary muscle fatigue is followed by rest and rebuilding. The exercise itself promotes aerobic effects — rich oxygenation of the blood, vigorous pumping of the heart, stimulated blood circulation to all parts of the body and movement of the lymph. As a result of systematic exercise, the daily energy supply increases, contributing to the sense of high-level well-being. This, however, is not what we usually call "fatigue."

What Happens in a Tired Body

Chronic fatigue is often a sign of approaching disease or a symptom of an existing one. But, before chronic fatigue sets in, there are many episodes of temporary fatigue, and we need to realize what is going on in the body when this happens.

In a state of fatigue, the body is being torn down faster than it is building up. At the micro-level, cells are unble to assimilate nutrients, create energy and rebuild themselves as rapidly as normal, and toxic metabolic wastes are backing up. Overuse of the nervous system creates enervation, poor nerve response. Nerve acids accumulate. Brain functions slow down. Catarrh and mucus back up on the lymph system and elsewhere in the body. Muscle cells lose their elasticity and cannot respond as rapidly or strongly; they are less capable of holding bones and ligaments in place. Membranes and epithelial tissue suffer loss of tone, becoming weaker.

Most ruptures occur in a fatigued body, and it is the most likely time for developing prolapsus of the transverse colon. The supportive tissue that holds the bowel in place becomes too flacid, too weak, to hold up the colon. A tired body is a likely candiate for back injury, hip injury, pulled muscles and torn ligaments since the muscle structure is too depleted to resist sudden stresses and strains. Digestion is poor. Loss of bowel tone slows elimination, and if there is a good deal of gas, diverticula may develop in the weakened bowel wall. Undigested or partly digested food is dumped into the bowel, increasing the waste load it must move. Assimilation through the bowel wall is inefficient. All elimination is slowed down through the lungs, kidneys,skin, lymphatic system, in addition to the bowel.

Circulating acids and toxins in the blood, lymph and interstitial fluid irritate tissues and may bring about inflammation in the inherently weak organs and tissues. Inflammation, of course, generates catarrh, which — if not eliminated properly — brings about a more advanced stage of inflammation. Inflammation, at the localized level, is tissue damage. If the catarrh is not moved along, eliminated, it invites germ life and viruses. Germ life and viruses cannot normally feed on living, healthy tissue. Rather, they are consumed by white blood cells, lymphocytes, antibodies — all the members of the natural immune system of the body. But, when they find a stagnant pocket of catarrhal waste, they feed on it and multiply by the billions, producing infection.

Infection, colds and flu are more common in a fatigued body because the natural immune system is depressed. The body is too busy coping with its own toxic metabolic waste to fight off sources of infection.

Meanwhile, because digestion and assimilation are impaired by fatigue, the body is slowed down in its recovery time. Fatigue can lead the body into a vicious, downward cycle of inflammation and disease if not checked promptly.

We must realize that the brain, slowed down by enervation, lack of nutrients and toxic waste buildup, becomes less efficient in directing and controlling the activities of the vital organs of the body. This, too, creates vulnerability to disease.

Studies have shown that after the age of 50, the average person loses 20% of his physical and mental abilities. When we consider the devasting effects of fatigue on top of that, it becomes evident how important it is to avoid conditions and situations that bring on fatigue and tiredness.

How Stars and Athletes Fight Fatigue

In a recent magazine article, comedienne Phyllis Diller was quoted as saying, "Happiness is a habit, and I have cultivated it . . . there's nothing for health like happiness." In addition to maintaining a good attitude, she eats a well-balanced diet, high in vegetables and low in meat; she avoids sugar and refined flour products.

David Doyle, star of "Charlie's Angels," says, "Once I gave up alcohol, I felt an incredible surge in my energy." Often, we don't realize how much energy is used up by the body to detoxify the "poisons" we put into our bodies through junk food, alcohol, smoking and drugs until we "kick the habit." Doyle also gets at least eight hours of sleep at night and eats well.

Red Buttons, film star and comedian, states, "I find the only time I'm really fatigued is when I'm sitting around thinking of my career— and not actively working on it." When we work at jobs that express our gifts and talents, we feel more vital, more energetic. Red Buttons can get by on very little sleep but he eats organic foods and takes supplements such as wheat germ oil and vitamin C.

Beautiful Adrienne Barbeau, who starred in the TV series, "Maude," and who appears often on TV shows, finds that fifteen-minute naps work well to restore her energy. She also uses a big glass of orange juice with honey as a "pickup."

Many film and TV stars have found that a demanding career can't be sustained on excessively rich eating habits, sugary foods, late night cocktail parties and other vitality wasting activities. Good food, positive attitudes and sufficient rest are as necessary for them as they are for all of us — perhaps more so.

In our time, we also find the more intelligent athletes, especially among the professionals, turning away from the "steak and potatoes" routine to focus on high-energy foods, vitality foods, foods that build the body without "undesirable side effects." Muhammed Ali remained world heavyweight boxing champion much longer than most have lasted because of special health supplements used during training and championship bouts. The greatest runners, bicyclists and Olympic athletes of our time are interested in foods and supplements that build the best body and the best performance possible. Stamina—the opposite to fatigue—is vital to athletic performance. Russian athletes and many others use vitammin B-15, calcium pangamate, for better oxygen utilization and stamina under the stress of performance. Special protein or carbo-hydrate drinks are being developed.

It is possible that injury-prone athletes may not take care of themselves as well as they should, allowing a combination of fatigue and inherent weaknesses to take them out of the game. One profesional basketball player with recurrent ankle problems didn't know that sodium was needed to keep the joints supple and strong. He would lose 15 pounds or more in perspiration per game, throwing off a great deal of sodium chloride. Depleted of sodium, fatigued by the tremendous physical demands of the game, his ankle couldn't hold up.

Chronic fatigue is unnecessary if we deal with particular instances of fatigue as they come up. Fatigue is a message from the body and mind, but we must be sensitive in interpreting it. Do we need rest? More food or better quality food? Vitamin and mineral supplements? Iodine for the thyroid? More exercise and fresh air? A change of jobs? We have to stop and think about these things to really understand how we can best respond to fatigue.

CHAPTER 4

MIND OVER DISEASE

How Mind Creates and Builds Disease

One of the laws that I feel is infallible, a law so conclusive and tangible that to see it happening and working is a phenomenon in itself, is this: the chemistry of man is altered with our thinking. I am convinced that what "issues from us" is actually what we live on.

There is a definite correspsondence between the functioning of the mind and the body, and the mind has the dominant role. Conscious life has its beginning within our own feelings; within our makeup and within what we make up; through what we imagine; what we hold in thought; what we perceive and conceive; what we judge and relate our lives to; how we include other people in our lives or leave them out; and how we push, pull and relate to people.

Psychosomatic Disease

The term "psychosomatic" comes from the Greek words *psyche,* meaning "mind and *soma* meaning "body;" it has come to represent conditions in the body which have originated in the mind. We all know that disease makes a person feel terrible, and it is not so surprising that Western medicine has begun to understand that the reverse can also be true; feeling terrible can lead to disease. Ulcers and colitis are obvious examples of the body-altering power of worry. Many other diseases, including cancer and arthritis, are believed now to have psychosomatic aspects.

Hate, fear, resentment, worry, anxiety, jealousy, anger, rage and other powerful negative emotions disrupt the glandular system and stimulate chemical changes in the body which may act exactly the same as toxins. In fact, the end results of such emotional releases are toxic. Many years ago, my mother told me, 'We must love others as ourselves not only for *their* good, but for *our own* good.'' She was right. Love is a healing activity; hate is a disease-producing activity.

Much has been said and written about stress as a factor in the development of disease. Modern living and working conditions are filled with stress-producing factors of all kinds. Many people choose to live in the ''fast lane'' of life, and high-speed living is undoubtedly dangerous to the health. But, I believe it is not stress but our response to it that determines whether it exerts a harmful or beneficial psychosomatic effect. Some people thrive on challenge, others shrink before it.

It is the hypothalamus of the brain where nerves stimulate the neurohormones which travel to the pituitary, the master gland of the body, and stimulate it to release other hormones which, in turn, affect other endocrine glands and body systems such as the heart, lungs, liver and muscles. Thoughts, feelings and perceptions, then affect every cell of the body. We can say, in a sense, that the hypothalamus is the ''stomach'' of the brain, and what we put into it has a direct relationship to our mental and physical health and level of well-being. We must be careful what we feed the mind.

Just as stasis in the body creates conditions for disease, so do bottled-up emotions. Everything in the body must move, everything in the mind must move: that is a law of well-being. The old must make way for the new. Compulsions, uncontrollable passions, for example, bring injury to the spleen. Worry and grief affect the functioning of the lungs, altering the breathing rate and depth of inhalation. Fear is hard on the kidneys and adrenals. Sadness weakens the heart tissues, and emotions of almost every kind affect the heart, for better or for worse. The thyroid, called the "emotional gland," is also responsive to feelings, and can be overtaxed by strong emotions. We find that anger and hate have effects upon the liver. When an organ is under emotional stress, its primary chemical elements are depleted very quickly. We know, for example, that B-compex vitamins are rapidly depleted under stress conditions, and, since the B vitamins mainly act as catylists for metabolic processes, it is clear that nutrients and chemical elements are being used up much faster than usual.

We must learn to digest, assimilate and excrete the "waste" of our mental experiences just as we process our food. We must have peace and harmony in the mind, which is where the spiritual domain comes into health. All great spiritual teachings emphasize letting go of regrets, disappointments, bad memories and the emotions that accompany them.

The Bible says, "As a man thinketh in his heart, so is he." What we hold to in our thought life becomes part of us. In England, a study of 10,000 cancer patients found the great majority to have been experiencing prolonged grief, hatred or resentment. These inharmonious mental states interfere with all life and lead directly to chronic and degenerative disease. The solution is to rid oneself of injurious mental activities, to learn to "forgive and forget," to "let go and let God," to stay away from spitty, spiteful people and seek the company of those who love us.

All the best foods cannot help a person whose digestive system is disturbed by mental turmoil.

Where do the influences on our minds come from? That is something to think about. What did our parents teach us about ourselves, about life? Was it positive or negative? How about school, friends, movies, TV? Have we been putting "junk food" into our heads as well as our bodies? Perhaps it's time for a change in diet. One of the things we must learn is to leave other people alone, to stop trying to tell others what to do, stop trying to remold our spouses into the image of what we want them to be. It is surprising how others around us change when we have changed our own attitudes and outlook. Learn to love people as they are.

The wonderful thing we can learn from psychosomatic disease is that if thoughts, perceptions and emotions can produce disease, they can also bring healing. That is a most powerful tool for anyone in the healing arts to know, and it should be standard equipment for all who believe in the wholistic approach. Health is a way of life, not just a matter of the right food, exercise and rest. The choices we make in the mind determine the path we take in life, so let's learn to make the right choices.

The Placebo Effect and Healing

Medical research in recent years has shown a great deal of interest in placebos — sugar pills or hypodermic injections of water given in place of drugs. The object is to fool the patient into thinking he has received real medication when, in fact, he has not. Studies have shown that many patients respond well to placebos.

One study showed significant improvement in mental hospital patients who were given pink sugar pills and were told they were a powerful new drug. Another study at the University of California in San Francisco was conducted with people who had their wisdom teeth taken out. Usually this involves considerable pain afterward. All were told they were being given pain-killing medication, but some were given only saline injections. Of these, one-third reported relief of pain. In other tests, placebos have been used with arthritis and asthma patients with a certain percentage of success in relieving symptoms.

Researchers have found that placebos can activate endorphins, naturally occurring chemical painkillers in the brain. In other cases, it has been suggested that placebos may activate glandular secretions or stimulate the body's natural immune system. What puzzles scientists is why placebos work on some people but not on others. One theory is that some persons are so naturally trusting and suggestible that their minds override the body functions and direct the body to respond as it would to a real drug.

Hypnosis has been used to heal many conditions, and it may be considered a type of placebo. I am not suggesting that ''fake'' healing takes place in the placebo effect but am simply pointing out that the mind seems to be in charge of the body's healing processes. One of the greatest medical hypnotists, Milton Erickson, noted that there were always some patients who refused, even under hypnosis, to allow healing to take place. We find, unfortunately, that there are people who want to hold onto their diseases.

While we tend to think of disease conditions as gradually building up outside of people's awareness, that may be only partially true. When doctors show kindness and concern for their patients, it is an established fact that healing is speeded up. On the other hand, it is certainly possible for people to bring on states of suffering and physical distress simply to get attention, kindness and concern from others. Those who feel unloved may sometimes make themselves sick just so they can get sympathy from relatives. One young woman related, "My mother in Chicago phones me at least three or four times a year to say how terrible she feels and how none of her children care enough to write and phone her more often. Doctors haven't been able to find anything wrong with her." This kind of thing happens more often than we think.

The placebo effect demonstrates one more way in which the mind exercises a great deal of control over health and disease. Norman Cousins, the famous one-time editor of *Saturday Review,* cured a serious degenerative disease called ankylosing spondylitis by watching funny movies and taking large amounts of vitamin C intravenously. Doctors had told him his chances of recovery were 1 in 500, but laughter showed they were wrong and brought complete healing. Mr. Cousins reported that ten minutes of belly laughter would give him two hours of pain-free sleep. Eventually, the combination of laughter, vitamin C and rest overcame the disease conditions in his body and drove them out. Several years after his healing, Norman Cousins was able to play golf and tennis and enjoy horseback riding, with no pain. Is it possible that the seriousness of his occupation over many years brought on the disease, and laughter was the main medicine he really needed?

We Have to "Feel Better" Before We Can Feel Better

Feeling flows along in the mind in very positive and negative ways. Positiveness works toward harmony. There is music that seems to be food to the ears and the heart, suitable to the deepest feelings a person has, right down to the deepest soul activity. A person has to feel good all the way through. To allow this good feeling to bathe the body takes care of the "dust of the earth" we have been talking about so much. However, the soul itself is beyond the "dust of the earth." It is not, itself, dust, but it moves dust. It "feeds" the dust, it puts our dust in order and, in that sense, it sustains this chemical body, readjusts and revitalizes it and puts it in the proper order.

The Healing Force Within

Psychologists tell us it has been proven that we control our emotions, and experience shows this is true. We can let our emotions control us—and some persons live that way—but it is healthier to learn to take charge. When I have faced "blue Mondays" and know that patients will be coming in, I have changed many times to a cheerful mood. I know my patients will respond better and get well faster if I am cheerful, so I break out of the doldrums because I want to help them.

How can we change our emotion? Simply by imagining or focusing our attention on something uplifting. Consider children and how easily they change emotions. A small child crying over a broken toy becomes joyful in an instant when mother says, "Grandma and Grandpa are coming over." All it takes is turning our attention to something we love or enjoy. I sometimes tell my patients, "You have to feel better to feel better," because feeling better must start in the mind before it can move into the physical body. This is the meaning of the first part of Hering's Law: "All cure starts from the head down. . . ." For this reason, I don't believe that depression can or should be taken care of from a drug standpoint, but rather from a disciplined change of attitude and a change in diet, as necessary.

The range and variety of feelings people experience is remarkable, and all have their effects upon the body. Yet, because we can control our feelings, we can avoid unhealthy states of mind by choosing healthy ones.

I am convinced that if we could tap into this wonderful healing force that is deep within us, we could readjust the physical ailments in our body and draw ourselves out of the depths of despair. We could avoid or alter moods of fear, anger, despair, hate and others of that kind, replacing them with a vibratory force to attract health and to maintain the "dust of the earth" that makes up our bodies in the proper physical and chemical order. By transforming disorganization to organization and "dis-harmony" to harmony, we would be able to transform "dis-ease" to ease. Well-being is within our reach if we use our spiritual and mental resources to acquire it.

V. G. Rocine believed this powerful healing force was available in the "Great Within." Emmett Fox taught that we must "stake our claim" in that area, proving that health "belongs" to us. This power is ours. It can be used as needed or desired.

I have seen my own body change when I changed my mind. I have observed my body work at a very low level of activity when I was unhappy, blue or influenced by a deteriorating environment. Similarly, I have watched yogi masters in India who had sufficient control over their bodies to be able to lift the hair on their arms at request, increase their blood pressure, slow their heartbeat. Under hypnosis, a man normally able to lift only 125 pounds was able to lift a 450-pound weight. An ordinary 5-foot 2-inch woman was involved in an auto accident in which her son was trapped under a station wagon. She lifted that car high enough so the boy could be removed. Normally, she could not have done it. But, the love she had for her son and the fear she experienced for his life gave her supernatural strength. Where did this power come from? It can produce miracles and yet, again, it lives in the electro-chemical activities of our body.

It is in these electro-chemical powers of our body that we have the capacity to heal and the power to change.

The Healing Power of Harmony

Disease is rightly named when we call it dis-ease. In contrast, it is harmony which must envelop the mind and body to create an atmosphere in which healing can follow along.

The basis for kinesiology is in the mind. The mind intuitively senses when the body is in disharmony with a particular substance, or when the body is deficient in certain chemicals, vitamins, enzymes and other nutrients.

I am convinced that the body is a servant to the mind and the spirit. However, we must serve that servant well; otherwise it will not be able to serve us well. Wherever we place our mind, whatever we put our attention on, grows and develops. It is well that we know that there is an energy working behind all physical material. Every ailment, every disease, is a symptom of something else that is hidden behind it. It is well that we look to see what is going on before the physical body reacts.

I have seen mounds of crutches in churches I have visited around the world. After healing experiences, people have left them, walking away whole. I have attended church services where people took off their glasses, having renewed their sight. Then, again, I have seen those who have come back after their crutches the next day and some even before because they didn't have the faith to hold what they had beheld in the beginning.

We have to recognize that the mind has ways to work in this physical body, ways that most of us don't know exist. It is a good thing to know that as we have a better liver we can have a better bowel. If we have a better bowel, we have a better lung structure. As we have a better lung structure, we have a better thyroid activity. Just as we see these various organs — one connected with the other, one needing the other and all working in harmony — we find that our thinking can also work in harmony to help us. It is not just a matter of logically working out one condition. It is a matter of joy, happiness, peace, harmony and showing forgiveness; a matter of blessing, being thankful, being grateful and putting the whole story together so that our whole body moves into a complete, healthy condition.

Whenever we have a heart condition, there is definitely a mental activity behind it. When we develop hate, the liver reacts to that. If we have a disappointment in love, we find that certain parts of our body are affected. We cannot breathe properly when we have been jilted or when we have experienced too much jealousy. Those words represent feelings, and we must know how to change one vibration into another. Otherwise, we cannot change the vibration of an ailment into a vibration representing a higher state of health.

In order to get rid of kidney trouble, we may have to go through a cleansing to get rid of resentment. I am convinced that we spend too much time on unhappy moments. Our bodies recognize this, and it shows when our minds are not working in the right direction.

We need a Universal Intelligence working through our body in order to bring harmony into our physical being. The electromagnetic impulses, the electrolytes that shift polarity in the nerve synapses, originate in our minds, whether we are at peace and ease or nurturing ill will or ill content.

Opening to Higher Potentials

We hear so much about taking certain drugs in order to keep going. People lean on these drugs, but if they must lean on something, why not a good thought? Why not on a higher, consciously chosen feeling, something real that can be called on any time? Something that does not leave "undesirable side effects."

We haven't learned to open ourselves to our higher potentials. Doctors definitely know that fear, hate, ill will and resentment produce acid conditions in the body which eventually break down our health reserves and natural defenses and eventually invite chemical changes that lead to disease, old age.

We had a lady at the Ranch one time who had a breast condition which had been diagnosed as cancer. She related a fascinating story which went far beyond coincidence. While working in the hospital as a nurse, a stainless steel table rolled across the kitchen, and the edge hit the affected breast. Two or three days later, she was going down the stairs in her home and hit the same breast on a bannister post. A few days later she hit the same breast on the corner of a chair. How can these things be brought into play? Why did she always hit the same breast? I wonder if her attention wasn't on that breast, somehow attracting those events? I sometimes think we have to get in and change what creates those conditions and seek our higher potentials.

The Great Within

The Great Within is where we should start in all of our healing. It is this Great Within that should be exalted and put on the highest level; it should be working in harmony with God so that, as this Great Within works with you, it is God working through you to accomplish that healing. There is a Great Within force that can take hold of a person and change him. A person can be healed within a week or two. As the Good Book says, a person can "change in the twinkling of an eye." We have met people whom we hardly recognize because of their attitude — their new attitude. On other occasions, we have seen people go downhill very fast.

I think the greatest object lesson I ever had was a lady who visited us two or three times describing how happy she was, how marvelous everything was, and how good this world was to her. But one day, she had a physical examination and was told she had cancer. I never saw that lady smile again; I never saw a bit of happiness come from her again. We find that here is where the body is leading the mind, and this is why I say that the physical and mental are working together constantly. It is to our advantage to get back to the Divine Mind that flows through us and let it lead the body. It may not be a complete cure but at least we owe it to ourselves to be good to ourselves and have the highest thoughts possible.

Where the Healing Begins

We have discussed changing the tissue structure of our body. We've described how old tissue is replaced by new as we balance the body chemistry through proper nutrition. We have considered stimulating the circulation to get the blood into the various tissues of our body. We have mentioned the need for improvement of our air, water and soil as a basis for trying to eliminate disease and bring mankind to a higher level of well-being. But I wonder if we realize there is also a definite replacement therapy for the mind, the old mental life making way for the new, setting off a spark of rejuvenation, new hope and new harmony. For instance, I feel that sometimes putting a new thought in place of an old one sparks a person to move in another direction to attract a different life for himself.

I believe that if we start reaching for a better type of relationship, especially with the people we associate with most often, the different thoughts that come to us as a consequence can give us ease and bring out new and productive principles to work by, a new creativity, a new walk, a new internal experience of life. Improved digestion can come into being just through changing our mind. As we ascend mentally, psychologically, spiritually, our body changes. And we find here that we are dealing with the most inner depths of our being. It is here that we start making a new path for ourselves, a way for our bodies to follow that will definitely create a true healing in the body.

To try to bring about healing entirely through the coarse physical methods we are working with today is a relatively primitive stage of the healing art. As we progress and move away from carrot juice therapy, and our thinking begins to raise our minds above all of our everyday, talk-about, walk-about problems, the first thing we will start to do is go within and seek a higher path with ourselves. We begin to put our mind and thinking on the higher talents. We recognize and start seeking a way of joy, of happiness, through making a change from "deep within" or, as I like to call it, the "secret place of the Most High."

We definitely know there is an effect of the mind upon the body. We definitely know that a person who lives in ease digests his foods better. We come to the place where we realize that it isn't what we eat that counts, it is what we digest that really promotes the best body. We recognize that every thought can get to every cell structure in our body. And we realize, as we progress further, that the body is a servant to the mind and spirit. If we can get to this place, we can get to a point of realizing where true healing takes place. We can get to the place where we realize that to be absent from the body is to be present with the law — the law of forgiving, the law of letting loose, the law of going unattached, the law of going free, happy and harmonious in life. And it is through this inner self being changed we find that the body follows, makes the changes and responds to whatever we have developed "within."

I am positive that hate, meanness and unforgiveness carried within a person are detrimental to the finer workings and the electromagnetic activity in the deeper cell structure of the body. When this is released, set straight, the acid conditions begin to leave, the ligament structures begin to receive better circulation — because of relaxation. This harmony begins to adjust the muscles to a more natural state of tension and to release a good deal of the acids locked up within the organs in the body.

If someone were to ask me, "Where do we start?" I would say that we have to start in our imagination. I believe that imagination is the strongest force in the world. I think it is the most powerful force we have at our disposal. Often our imaginations roam at random over unhealthy and destructive images. Yet, I feel if it was put under control, we could permanently direct more of what is going on in our body and bring about desirable physiological changes. Imagination is capable of triggering off some of the greatest healing that can possibly come about. And we start from the "deep within."

Imagination — A Vital Cure Start in Life

Imagination, as I have said, is the greatest force we have in this world. However, in looking at imagination, it can be used for good and it can be used for harm. The substance of our imagination is the picture we hold before our mind. We have an opportunity to outpicture what we may call the thought form that we have created in the past moment. As this new picture comes upon us, we either accept it and control it, or lose it and let it go. It is right there that we can choose to allow imagination to become real life.

Imagination can go in any direction. It is not considered real until we bring it into action. We take it on, believe in it, live it, produce from it, act for it, act with it, live in it, know that it is so. It may come to us in the form of fears. It may come to us in the form of ecstasy. It may come to us in the form of a harmonious living moment. It comes to us in enlightenment. It comes to us in a moment of necessity for relief. When we allow imagination to dwell on negative thought forms, these are outpictured. It may bring us hate. It may bring us into creation of violence. It can bring on temper. Or, it may bring on fatigue, tiredness — the preconditions of disease.

It is here that we recognize the power of mental pictures. Reality comes into existence as our thought life generates physical change and action. We live in pictures, in this sense. That's why I say we have to outpicture that which we have accepted in the past.

Many live in their imaginations. Many experience "figments of their imaginations," as it has been said. It's all in your mind; it's all in your head; it's all in your imagination. If we could realize that careful study of the imagination could teach us ways to avoid or overcome disease and to achieve good health, we would have access to one of the most powerful tools for triggering off a healing process in the body.

I have closely studied the writings of Emil Coue, a French psychoanalyst and suggestive therapist, who awakened me to the fact that disease responds to the suggestions that we give ourselves, the suggestions that come from other people, the kind of picture we make of ourselves, the kind of picture we accept as other people give us suggestions. To a great extent, the effectiveness of hypnosis depends upon the extent of our mental assent to the suggestions of the hypnotist. Life itself repeatedly involves a similar kind of assent or trust as we build our future by focusing on and believing in certain events and not others. We find that suggestion is brought to us in the form of fears we may imagine about tomorrow, fear of taking on a new job, fear of failure in marriage, fear of speaking before the public, fear of stuttering. The basis of many of our diseases today could be traced back to the fact that we have allowed our imagination to receive them first. To recover and leave disease behind, this has to be changed, and we have to go in another direction.

It was Emil Coue who said, "Day by day, in every way, I am getting better and better." When you stop and think about it, many people know they are sick. They have claimed it. We encounter a lot of people who "know" they're going to be sick, and they're expecting it. It has been said in the Good Book that what we fear comes upon us. We find that through our suggestions, through our imaginations, we attract more pictures, a bigger problem or a better way of getting out of our problems. It is the person who has cleared his mind and has taken on the path of positive imagery good for his body who is going to trigger of the "getting well" process as we know it to start from the "deep within."

I have learned that exalting the "great within," bringing it to a harmonious state, one the body can accept, one the body needs, one the body is hoping for, one the body can mold to easily, can give us deeply satisfying rest, the kind that those who are weary and heavy laden have built up in that "deep within." We talk about people who have mental blocks. We find these can be traced to some type of imaginary experience of a problem. It is actually not as big as we imagined it to be. Or, it may not be a real problem. Yet, when we take on this imaginary problem, a disturbance develops within and distorts our body, interferes with the digestion, upsets our heartbeat, alters the secretions and the hormone balance in our body.

Many a person could be released from sexual problems, from fatigue and tiredness, from mental problems that have a direct effect on all organs in the body. It is very difficult to find the cause of many of these problems, as the psychoanalyst knows. And, of course, nobody goes around with a psychoanalyst at his side constantly. But, we have the opportunity being our own psychoanalysts, our own suggestive therapists, the one who can right wrongs when we find the truth of the matter. We can begin to live a life of health, of freedom from anxiety, through "changing our minds."

How many times have we heard the statements, "He worried himself sick," or "He has a chip on his shoulder?" We have people who actually want to hurt people to get revenge, and this is what they carry in their minds. We encounter people who feel that they must get even with people, perhaps because of something said the previous week. They are unwilling or unable to get it off of their minds. It is in the imagery department of our mind that the seeds of disease or well-being are planted.

When we deal with the chemistry of our body, we need to recognize that there is also a mental chemistry that goes on in the mind. Like the body, the mind may be deficient in certain "elements" or toxic laden or underactive. To balance the mental chemistry, there is thought chemistry, there is suggestive therapy chemistry, there is a "mind over matter" chemistry that we can use to restore health and balance.

For us to only consider foods, exercise, chiropractic or mechanical treatments, we have to leave out the mind, the most vital part of the body. Who wants to have a physical body and no love in their heart? Who wants to go through life married to a man who has no thought of your happiness besides keeping you as a good sex partner? Who wants to limit life and its meaning to the purely physical level with no love or harmony developed in other departments of life?

Doctors and others interested in human potential on the verge of discovering now that we are vibrant beings, that we are very deep and complex beings in our thoughts and in the ways we express ourselves. That which is within also expresses without. That which is above can also come below and develop within. We find there can be a heaven here on earth. Yes, in the little ten acres we call a human body, if we can only imagine what that heaven can be, and if we could once only feel it and know its effects, then I think we would never want to go back. Very few people know what it is to feel wonderful. Most people are going through life just taking on whatever life gives them. The average person today doesn't have a well-developed imagination, one that is practical, one that doesn't live constantly in fantasies that dissipate or negate the pure and wonderful and beautiful possibilities of life.

We have to consider that the imagination is a mental department all its own. Some people can form pictures that are just unbelievable. They are capable of going from one picture to another. Imagination, of course, can be the basis for lying, for stealing, for criminality. When we believe a lie, we live a lie. It can also be used in the other direction, with an extreme emphasis on truth. My father wanted to have truth expressed in the family so much that we children were under constant surveillance. We were constantly watched to make sure we did the right thing. If we told a lie or if we did the wrong thing, according to the way he saw it, we were almost beaten to a pulp. As children, we lived in fear. We developed a fearful picture of our own father, one where love couldn't come in and take its place. Imagination is something that we can use to bring a family together. It can also break a family up.

It is essential to work with productive imagery with pictures that are going to be good for us. Imagination can be used in our government. It can be used in healing. It can be used in our jobs. It can be used in our marriages. There isn't any place we go where we can't hold this new picture always ahead of us. And it's one of our own self-creation. We find that in that self-creativity we have to be grounded in the humanities, how to treat people, how to forgive and forget.

How much should we keep in our mind? Have you been keeping something on your mind too long? Is it something that is eating you? And, what is it that you take to bed with you? Do you have problems and troubles that are necessary to carry? What is so necessary about them? Is it possible that you could make a change in your life in the image department? I think it would be well for you to consider that controlling our imagery is a high priority in life.

We would like to make some suggestions here from the standpoint of maxims or aphorisms, things that we can believe in, ways of changing our mind and doing something for internal healing. We know that certain changes are going to take place, that what we put into the imagination is going to change our consciousness which, in turn, will finally change the physical body, the outer expression of the self. I believe very much that healing in itself — not doctoring but healing — begins in changing the consciousness of man. I tell my patients, when we change our consciousness, we can get out of our sickness. So it almost looks like we have to start with the mind. To be honest about what I believe from the healing standpoint, I would say that the true chemistry of man starts ''deep within'' a person.

Aphorisms or Axioms To Believe In

1. Nothing can disturb you unless you give it your consent.
2. If the outlook isn't good, get a new outlook.
3. Fear is faith working backwards.
4. Nothing is worth disturbing you if it brings on ill health.
5. We should study very deeply the following saying of the Good Book: ''For God hath not given us the spirit of fear; but of

power, and of love, and of a sound mind." Stop and think about what you can do with this in mind.

6. There are no birds in last year's nest.
7. God created food for the birds but He didn't put it in their nests.
8. Do not seek the happiness you want in another person.
9. Let people go; the experiences they're about to have they may need.

MURPHY'S LAW OF RANDOM PERVERSITY

Basic Law: "If Anything Can Go Wrong, It Will."

Addenda & Variations

★ Left to themselves, things go from bad to worse (Murphy's law of administration entropy).

★ If you explain something so clearly that no one can possibly misunderstand it, someone will.

★ If there is a possibility of several things going wrong, the one that will go wrong is the one that will do the most damage.

★ Nature always sides with the hidden flaw.

★ If you play with a thing long enough, you will surely break it.

★ If everything appears to be going well, you have obviously overlooked something.

★ Nothing is ever as simple as it first seems.

★ It is easier to get into a thing than out of it.

★ Whatever you want to do, you have to do something else first.

★ If you try to please everybody, somebody is not going to like it.

★ There are some problems that only a good funeral can solve.

CHAPTER 5

VITAL FORCE AND VITALITY WASTERS

When healing begins to take place, we know the vital force is returning to the patient. Iridology, the analysis of the eyes, reveals white healing lines in the iris at this point, visible evidence of the return of the vital energy. Tissue cannot rejuvenate unless the vital force is there to bring about regeneration.

We can pick up a certain amount of vital force and energy through foods and exercise but we also need plenty of rest and sufficient recreation. Otherwise we remain fatigued, dull, lethargic. To a great extent, the vital energy or lack of it, depends on the mental life and the spiritual life. We cannot focus on bad memories; we cannot work for Tension Corp.; and we cannot carry anger, hate, jealousy and bitterness. If we do, we find that the body wears out faster than we can build it up. So, it is a physical, mental and spiritual thing. We have to get rid of confusion, anxiety, resentment and antagonism, because they are vitality wasters. You have to know better in order to feel better.

Friendships are important. Vital energy is wasted among people who only criticize, complain and throw verbal garbage. Vital energy is wasted around people who do not like you. Stay away from them. Work out the marriage problem and get on with life. We need love and joy to feed the vital force, the vital energy.

One of my patients, an 80-year-old woman, had two men come to her house and demand payment for a roofing job she knew she had already paid for. She became very upset and told them she had a receipt to prove she had paid. "We don't care what you have," one of them said. "We're going to come into your house and stay until you pay us." They scared her so much she had a stroke. Keep in mind that this was purely a mental thing.

Our thoughts and emotions profoundly affect our health. We live in these mental things that come upon us. When a person has done all he can physically, it is best for him to sit down and get hold of the mental and spiritual thing.

Now, when the doctor has taken care of the physical and mechanical problems of the patient, is the job over? No. We need to lead the patient to higher ground. We need to lead him to the higher path. I don't mean push him, pull him or carry him — I mean *lead him*. They said God can only do for you what He can do through you. Is the consciousness of the patient attracting negative things? Then he needs to change his attitude — literally, change his mind. It is said, "Beauty is in the eye of the beholder." The rose is in the eye of the beholder. And, church is not so much a building as a condition of heart and attitude.

The universe is a wonderful, beautiful place, full of riches for the seeker. But, we find we cannot see its beauty or its riches if our eyes are looking down. We have to look up.

Experience flows and changes. Truth is eternal. We can learn new truths but we can never change old ones, because truth remains the same. So, we use truth as a beacon, a light, to guide us on the path. I'm not trying to convey spiritual principles here, but rather to show in a most practical way that these things are very important in health and disease.

In ancient times, the philosopher Pythagoras taught that existence was characterized by ten pairs of opposites. He talked about light and darkness, good and evil, rest and motion, male and female and so on. We find we belong to one or the other, and there are times when we must go within to straighten out what we are experiencing on the outside. The vital force we have within us is related to what we are picking up in life, what we are attracting to ourselves by the male and female principles inside us.

To understand what is going on in the sex life of a person, we have to look further than sexual performance. What is the inheritance from the mother and father? What is on the person's mind? Is there a strain to find the female principle within yourself, or to find the male to match the male principle? We find this is a vibrational process, and it can become bottled up on the inside.

Vital force always moves with the vibratory principle. It always breaks down into what you have brought with you from your mother and father — strengths and weaknesses, positives and negatives, gifts and handicaps, potential for giving and receiving. I am not saying you are totally limited by your inheritance, but this is the starting place. We always start with where we are, who we are now. There is a vibratory quality to color, to foods, to places. A dog doesn't always sleep where a cat sleeps. How we feel can be influenced by whether underground water flows beneath our home. The Chinese know a great deal about these things.

A nurse told me not long ago of a child who had a problem with bedwetting. While rearranging the furniture in his room, she turned the bed with the head toward the north. Now, this was not done intentionally, but she found the child stopped wetting the bed in less than a week. Something to think about, isn't it?

Diseases have their own vibratory rate. So do personalities. Each of us has his or her own color, tone, rhythm to express. We become emotionally fulfilled by meeting the needs of others. It is more blessed to give than to receive, so the saying goes. But, if we refuse to receive a gift, do you realize we are denying a blessing to the giver? We must receive as well as give.

To heal a dis-ease, it is best to muster all possible vital energy from all sources in the universe available to us. Healing does not take place in the hospital room any more than reform takes place in a jail cell. In both cases, the person is there because of the consequences of his actions. To get out of either place, it is necessary to do some changing, which takes vital force.

When Hippocrates said, "Give me a fever and I will cure any disease," do you think he was talking merely about burning up toxic wastes? Think about it. Hippocrates was a wise man. He didn't mean we could heal a disease by getting into a sauna or steam bath and sweating it out. To him, the heat generated to give rise to a fever was a demonstration of the vital force coming up in the body to throw off disease. That is what he wanted to see, the vital force moving from the inside out. He called it a sacred force because of its wonderful results in healing.

We can extend this further by going to Hering's Law of Cure, which says, "All cure comes from the head down, from the inside out, and in reverse order as the symptoms first appeared." The vital force develops first in the mind and spirit, moving down into the body to strengthen the vital organs and activate the healing process before expanding outward in the body, heating and burning up toxic deposits and ridding the body of them. The elimination of toxic wastes proceeds in reverse chronological order, bringing back old symptoms — the most recent ones first — as the tissue is cleansed and rejuvenated. It is basically a vibratory process in which spirit, mind and body all cooperate, casting out the old disease vibration to make way for the new vibration of well-being. Old psychological problems and memories often come up in this process which is called a healing crisis. They, too, are cast out along with catarrhal and chemical toxins. The spirit is cleansed, the mind is cleansed, the body is cleansed. And, the power to accomplish this comes from the vital force, the vital energy.

No one gets well without vital force. you can provide a patient with the right foods, the right chiropractic adjustments, use the right acupressure points and massage. But, if his mind and spirit are not in vibrational harmony with what is being done at the physical level, he will be tearing down the vital energy faster than you can build it up. We are discussing the wholistic approach here, the treatment of the whole man. You can't treat only a kidney, a heart problem or a respiratory condition. Think about it — 90% of the person is on the other end of that problem. You must take care of the whole person.

Vital force is the energizer for motivation. Vital force provides the power to think, feel, act. The presence or absence of vital force determines whether we are lion-hearted or chicken-hearted. The soul precedes the mind in order of existence, and it uses the body to create certain experiences for learning purposes. We can no more hold our bodies permanently than we can hold experiences. Life is flow; the body is flow. New skin cells develop on the hands every 24 hours. You can't keep the old skin. New blood cells replace the old every 120 days. The body we have now is not the same one we had a decade ago, a year ago, a day ago or even a second ago. The mind and body are an expression of the soul.

Growth comes through obstacles, through lessons. Life is simple, but it isn't easy. You may take on a marriage for growth reasons and have children for purposes of growth. With the right attitudes and the right spiritual approach, you will learn your lessons and go on. It is when we refuse to face obstacles, refuse to learn lessons, that our vital force is depleted. Some people feel they have married the wrong person, or that the person they married ten years ago has changed into someone they no longer appreciate. Some people feel their children wear them out. Are we learning our lessons or are we fighting them? Are we building our vital energy or losing it?

When we first marry, we are involved with emotions and the sexual expression. We must realize that the soul isn't going to stay in these places forever. There are deeper avenues of growth the soul needs in order to develop. There are brain faculties lying dormant that the soul wants awakened and energized. In my book, **Iridology, Volume II,** I go into the brain centers and expressions in detail, and when we consider the complexity of the human nervous system, we can see we are an "instrument of a million strings."

What does it mean to be an instrument of a million strings? Let's go back to Pythagoras for a moment. Pythagoras discovered that if you plucked a string on a harp, the strings exactly an octave above and below that string would vibrate sympathetically. Our perceptions operate according to this principle of sympathetic vibration. We communicate — or fail to communicate — with others by reason of the same principle. We love some things and detest other things.

We respond to vibration every moment all of our lives. We find it in color, heat, sound, electricity, movement, our heartbeat—everywhere. And, we are designed to respond to it. Our body, mind, soul and spirit are designed to respond to vibrations and to affect one another in so doing.

Pythagoras believed that the object of life was to attune ourselves with the vibrations around us, to come into harmony with the universe. We learn from disharmony as well as harmony. We may have inherited many problems from father and mother, but they are given to us for soul growth, not to create misery. We need obstacles to overcome to help us learn and grow. It isn't necessary to see problems as an invitation to combat. That isn't what they are for. Stay calm. Understand what it is. Then overcome it. Disease is an obstacle, not an enemy. Use it to learn from. Use it to learn about healing, to learn about finding a right way to live.

We cannot say, "I am sick," and believe it without getting sick. Why? Because we live on our beliefs. We walk on our beliefs. We follow them and meet certain consequences on the path. The body is servant to the mind and the spirit, and when we tell the body it is sick, the vital force draws back and allows it.

The Mayo Clinic says that 9 out of 10 people with stomach ulcers got them from fretting, stewing and worrying — mostly over love troubles and money problems. The experts say an operation takes 10 years off a person's life. They tell us that birth control pills reduce a woman's mental acuity by 10%. Negative things are all around us, but we have the power to choose not to take them in.

We find it is in our attitudes, thoughts and beliefs that we become a vitality waster. We don't balance our lives; we don't go to the place where we can see the nicer things in life.

Disharmony is always an invitation to harmony and at the same time a signal that something is wrong. A person who lives in the "blues" lives in dejection and depression. These are vitality wasters. If we knew what joy could do to build up our energies, we would seek it instead of settling into lower-level expressions.

The color red can bring courage and confidence. Being in the presence of some colors changes our attitude, awareness, thinking, spiritual expression. We can't stay in the blues. We must move along.

We should not remain in those vibrational states in which all that money was lost, the car broke down, there was death in the family, friendships lost, the dog died — depression, mourning, sorrow— drawing out all the vitality in the body.

The shortest sentence in the Bible is, "Jesus wept."

He got over it quickly and back to his Father's business again. That's the way. Make it short and move right along. There are many people mourning for things, events, people who have passed on. Leave it to God. Leave it to God to take care of those things and get on with your work.

We don't catch dis-ease, we earn it. We don't fall into dis-harmony, we create it by being disharmonious. The universal symptom of disease and disharmony is fatigue, and fatigue is either cause or effect when we consider the emotional states that precede or follow it. There are certain low-level mental states that we can characterize as vitality wasters. The following list is taken from my recent book, **Iridology: Volume II.**

VITALITY WASTERS

Inefficiency	Dishonesty	Carelessness	Indiscriminate sex
Uncertainty	Embarrassment	Terror	Brutality
Evasiveness	Indiscretion	Uneasiness	Obsessions
Quibbling	Apathy	Disrespect	Hallucinations
Equivocation	Disinterestedness	Antipathy	Phobias
Mistakenness	Leniency	Scorn	Harshness
Indecisiveness	Laxity	Spitefulness	Greed
Disharmony	Morbidity	Boredom	Selfishness
Impatience	Stupidity	Viciousness	Indolence
Short-sightedness	Hate	Bad temper	Coerciveness
Imitation	Laziness	Agony	Cruelty
Triteness	Confusion	Callousness	Destructiveness
Competitiveness	Destructiveness	Neuroses	Arbitrariness
Envy	Gives up easily	Psychoses	Anxiety
Jealousy	Weakness	Impulsiveness	Worry
Fear of opposite sex	Aversion	Intolerance	Fear
Dullness	Grief	Forgetfulness	Intolerance
Misunderstanding	Contempt	Stuttering	Rage
Distractability	Malice	Confusion	Tyranny
Stubbornness	Humiliation	Vengefulness	Imprudence
Over-seriousness	Doubt	Arrogance	Perfunctoriness
Vanity	Sadness	Infantalism	Bullying
Clownishness	Tragedy	Loneliness	Forgetfulness
Duplicity	Misery	Frigidity	Evasiveness
Lying	Unfriendliness	Disinterest	Restlessness
Deceitfulness	Dependency	Insanity	Insomnia
			Nervousness

These are the things we must deal with in our patients. Our bodies are made from a certain weave of cloth at birth. Life is a process of learning how to wear that cloth, how to make lovely clothing from it. We must learn to help our patients understand that the body follows the mind and spirit. Then we must help them learn to use their mental and spiritual resources to lead the body up the higher path.

According to Hering's Law, if we change what is in the mind, the change will come down into the body. If we change what is in the inside, that change will express on the outside. As we move into the new life, the old life will be cast off and discarded, like a worn-out coat.

Many who seek to overcome health problems are working at the level of carrot juice. They are working at the level of food combinations. What they really need to be working on is mental combinations, the harmonizing of the vibrations at the mental and spiritual level. This is how we free the vital force to do its work in the body. This is how we get on the path to healing and continue on to high-level well-being.

CHAPTER 6

DO DRUGS BELONG IN YOUR BODY?

There is a more or less new twist in advertising these days. People seem to be falling for one of the greatest hoaxes ever attempted. That is, when we go into drug stores or supermarkets and there is what they refer to as the "Health Aids" section. It consists of all the over-the-counter drugs used to take care of and relieve the colds, flus, fevers, pains and aches of the various organs that are discharging or hurting. There are shelves full of remedies for fevers, sneezing, coughing, headaches, and irritations of the skin. I would consider this more of a Cosmetic Department than a Health Aids section.

When we are patching up, salving over and covering up symptoms; we aren't restoring health; we're covering up health problems. We are not getting rid of the headache causes when we take a pain reliever, and even if it's three times the strength it was some years ago, it's not going to rebuild tissue, fortify the blood stream or replace lost vitamins and minerals in the body.

Some years ago, I saw a report of the previous year's partial drug consumption in the U.S. That year, Americans used 37,273,000 pounds of aspirin, 4,037,000 pounds of penicillin, 1,541,00 pounds of tranquilizers and 836,000 pounds of barbiturates. This comes to 21,844 tons of drugs and that is only part of the total. The report I saw wasn't complete — but it was complete enough.

We continue in lifestyles that hamper the ability of the organs in the body to function. By poor food choices and bad exercise habits, we break down the integrity of the tissue. Then we turn to mouthwashes to get rid of the bad breath, take fever reducers, pain relivers and use a couple of squirts of nasal decongestant. We don't think of letting the mucus drain. We don't consider our diet. We haven't put the time and energy into learning about the role of nutrition in the prevention of disease, nor is it taught in our institutions of higher education as a means of healing our bodies of illnesses. The doctors do not pay attention to the science of balancing the chemical elements in the human body and what the chemical story can do for us. We are neglecting the needs of the human body.

When we are having sinus troubles we take care of that from a drainage standpoint, but we neglect the bowels, the lungs and all the other organs that are contributing to that problem.

When we can't sleep very well, we get nighttime sleep-aid pills. When we have aches and pains in our legs we get arch supports, a heel lift, different types of shoes. If we have a bad meal, we go for an antacid. We buy Crest and treat our gums from the outside. And now Tums come along and they've added calcium. I wonder if people realize what kind of calcium they are getting there.

We take care of the acids with Alka-Seltzer. One place we saw in Miami advertised free Alka-Seltzer with each meal. Is it possible that we would eat in such a way that we have to have an Alka-Seltzer guarantee to go with the meal? What does it do for you besides offer temporary relief?

Many people really don't know where to eat, how to eat or what to eat. They don't know that the food they put in their mouth is going to have an effect on every organ in the body. Maybe they won't see that effect today, but they will over a period of time if they continue to suppress every single symptom with some sort of quick-relief remedy.

A young man may find his skin breaking out. He never used to have this trouble, but now he has it. The television ads claim their creams dry the pimple from the inside out, but neglect to point out that diet is one of the crucial factors in maintaining a clear skin. Yet, they would have you believe it can be fully controlled by surface treatments.

Most of us are not getting the proper amount of exercise. We are not getting the proper silicon material in our chemical balance. The skin is a storage house for silicon and without it we cannot be well. All degerminated foods are lacking in silicon. Silicon was there to begin with in the natural foods, but then we began to use all kinds of formulas, instant foods and preserved foods along with drugs.

When something is needed for our dry skin, many use Vaseline, practically a household name, not realizing that Vaseline is a coal tar product and through the absorption of this over a period of years, we could have a suppression develop that will most likely cause side effects in some other area of the body.

Then we have all of the different cough and cold suppressants that are found on the shelves of the health sections in these various stores. It seems it shouldn't be called the health aid section, it should be called the relief section, because all these drugs really do is just provide momentary relief.

Does anyone realize that it takes cancer twenty years to develop? Wouldn't you think that the body would give us some indication of a problem within that time span? It tries to, but we don't respond, we just "take something" for it.

We are hearing a lot of commercials about fiber and bulk these days, and one is always claiming to be so much better than any other leading product, but where does that leave the public in terms of correct information?

Now we have the caffeine-free products. All of a sudden they find out that caffeine is bad for us and so there is a whole string of caffeine-free products. But, this doesn't make the rest of the product good for you. In fact, removing the caffeine has been claimed to leave a harmful chemical residue.

Then we resort to douches, ear drops, cough syrups and pain relievers that contain hydrocortisone, all relief measures. We go from aspirin to nighttime cold formulas, and yet researchers admit there is no cure for the cold and all we can do is get relief for it.

Why don't we look for the cause? Why don't we look for some way of creating change in our lives and of building good bodies? We are lost in a maze of advertisements today, brainwashed, not realizing that there is so much more to take care of.

This is one of the worst things that I believe has been perpetrated on the public today. This is not a health program, this is a drug program and should be advertised as such. There's no reason they should say that they are doing anything for your health. Ninety percent of this advertising is done without a doctor's approval and sixty percent of the money that is made on drugs is spent for more advertising.

Maybe I am not supposed to tell a person or industry not to do this because I'm stepping on the freedom and privacy of the drug manufacturers. Yet here we are, living in the various stages of drug consciousness, drug after-effects and drug residues in our tissues. Multitudes of people are being diagnosed as terminal every day, and in my work I have seen the cleansing results of wholistic treatment, I have seen chronic conditions reverse, and it is terribly difficult to sit quietly and watch people suffer due to their ignorance of facts.

We have become a nation of caretakers and we will continue to be until the facts are brought to light and vibrant health becomes our goal.

The waiting room in the doctor's office is not waiting to tell you how to prevent disease, that waiting room is waiting to tell you that you have a chronic, or worse yet, a degenerative disease. Are doctors curing heart trouble? Are doctors curing multiple sclerosis? Are they curing cancer? No, they are not. They are just learning new modes of disease management.

We have stimulants, depressants and mood regulators. We have the sedatives and tranquilizers, and those that take these drugs end up as patients with very complicated problems, mental and physical.

Prescription and over-the-counter drugs are only part of the problem. Children and young adults, raised in a drug-oriented society, see no reason not to freely indulge in the drug craze, using marijuana, speed, halucinogenics, and anything they can get their hands on. An 8-year study by UCLA psychologists showed that teenagers who abuse hard drugs like cocaine, heroin and Quaaludes are less likely to finish high school, and more likely to have unsuccessful marriages and relationships. The group of teens studied showed that drug abusers had more problems, committed more crimes and were more suicidal. We have to remember that drugs often have genetic effects that are carried on into the next generation.

Diethylstilbestrol (DES) a cancer-causing agent, is still being found in some meat, despite its illegality. Profit-minded farmers use it to boost cattle weight cheaply. Sulfamethazine is given to pigs and cattle to reduce bacterial infections and sickness, and residues are showing up in the pork, veal and milk sold in markets. Sulfamethazine has caused cancer in laboratory rats and mice. DDT, banned in the U.S., is being found in imported beef used in fast food outlets. All such drugs in meat may cause cancer and genetic damage and should be strictly forbidden.

Is the government soft on dangerous drugs? In 1988, the U.S. Food and Drug Administration decided not to restrict the use of sulfite drugs on foods, despite the fact that over a dozen people, allergic to the sulfite, have died from it. The Center for Science in the Public Interest says that as many as a million persons could be endangered by exposure to sulfites. Perhaps that's not as bad as the government's attitude toward nicotine and smoking, which is known to cause cancer and emphysema, and contributes to heart disease. Surgeon General C. Everett Koop has said that nicotine is an addictive drug, nevertheless, the U.S. government continues to tolerate this multi-billion dollar industry, despite the billions U.S. taxpayers must pay in medical bills of those who get cancer, emphysema and heart disease but who don't have the money to pay.

We should certainly hope that in the future there will be restraint and regulations that distinguish what is health-producing and what is disease-producing before anyone ingests it into their system.

If we place any value on the quality of our lives, we are going to have to recognize the difference between living within the natural laws as opposed to buying some kind of chemical remedy that makes the problem worse.

There are times when we need the drugs, when there's an urgency and a person really needs assistance. But, chronic use of drugs is something we have to exercise caution about and really discern whether we are taking a health path.

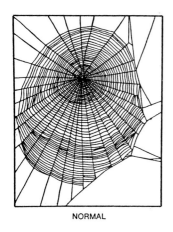

NORMAL

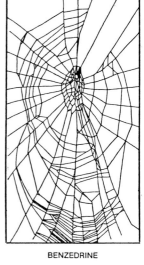

BENZEDRINE

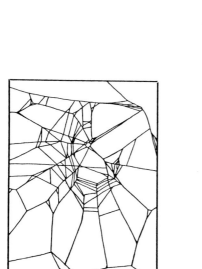

CAFFEINE

Drugs alter our thinking, perception and behavior, just as they altered this spider's ability to spin a good web. Caffeine, used so casually by millions, is an addictive drug that impairs thinking and interferes with liver function when used regularly.

79

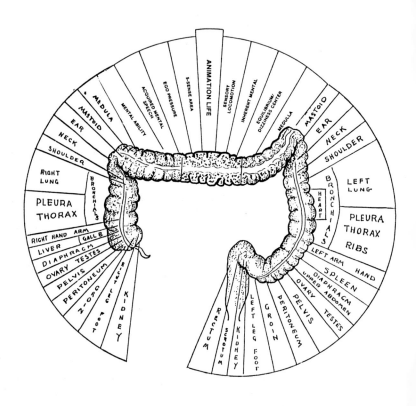

The neural reflex arc is a genetic connection between inherent weaknesses in the colon and organs, glands and tissues in the body. Notice how the chart shows the relationship of many body parts to the colon. If a chronic or degenerative condition is triggered in the bowel, a similar reflex condition, also chronic or degenerative, is triggered in the part of the body to which the colon reflexes.

80

CHAPTER 7

TAKING CARE OF YOUR LYMPH SYSTEM

It is interesting to consider that we have three times the volume of lymph in our bodies than blood, and that the lymphatic system circulates through its own independent system of vessels. It is as separate a system as the gastrointestinal system. Lymph fluid is light and volatile, it acts like gas in its ability to penetrate the most difficult, hard-to-reach parts of the body, such as the joints, ligaments and even the lens of the eye. It penetrates tissue where blood can never enter.

Unlike the blood circulatory system, the lymph system doesn't have a pump, such as the heart, to move the lymph along. The lymph is moved along the vessels by the movement of muscles, not only by exercise, but by breathing movement as well. Lymph vessels have delicate walls that collapse easily. The lymph goes only in one direction because of a series of one-way valves, and eventually ends up emptying into the blood veins near the heart. The lymph flows one direction only — from the outermost parts of the body, through the muscles, organs, glands and tissues, finally joining the blood.

Lymph is involved in the repair of our tooth structure. The tooth substance is made up of a calcium compound called dentin, which must be replaced periodically. We also have a lens in the eye which must be replaced periodically. We also have a lens in the eye which must have nutrients brought in and wastes carried away. Eye lens tissue is alive, constantly breaking down, repairing, rejuvenating and rebuilding. It's calcium metabolism becomes upset when we are exposed to too much stress or follow an imbalanced food routine. Cataracts develop in an inactive lens structure that does not have the proper mineral balance. When we stop and think about it, the penetration of this particular organ in the body can *only* be by the lymph system.

The gastrointestinal system, which functions almost independently of the rest of the body, is connected to the body only by the blood, lymph and nerves. The nerves control the peristaltic and digestive motions of the stomach and bowel while the blood carries nutrients and oxygen to the tissues and takes away wastes and carbon dioxide. Lymph does nearly everything the blood does, except to participate in oxygen/carbon dioxide exchange. Sodium is the dominant chemical element in lymph, which is similar to a salty blood plasma — the clear portion of the blood. Both blood and lymph are essential fluids.

The lymph system carries unstable chemicals such as iodine, chlorine and fluorine. Iodine is the metabolizer in the body, water soluble and noted for penetrating tissues that only the finest fluids can go through. Chlorine is a cleanser and fluorine is an antiseptic and bone-hardening agent. There are many tissues blood can never penetrate because it is relatively thick. Fluorine in foods is very unstable. If it is exposed to too much heat, fluorine will evaporate.

The fluorine carried by the lymph system is called the disease-resistant element. Fluorine is also valued by the medical and dental profession because they say it hardens the bones and teeth and makes them more durable. The teeth, they say, have fewer cavities. Those who oppose the use of fluoridated water, toothpaste, etc., say that fluorine, in any amount, damages the thyroid, especially when the thyroid is deficient in iodine. Since the thyroid has such a broad range of effects on the rest of the endocrine system and on the metabolism, any thyroid damage should be avoided, if at all possible.

I believe that fluoride acts as an antiseptic in the lymph system.

Where is fluorine found? It is in raw foods, raw milk, vegetables, whole grains, seeds and nuts. However, it is driven out if the foods have been cooked. It is difficult to find this elusive element, fluorine, in foods. Three out of five people are troubled with joint deposits due to insufficient fluorine. Fluorine is found on the outsides of the bones. Disease and decay cannot exist in the presence of fluorine and yet again, it is such an elusive element that the lymph is the only fluid in the body that can carry it.

The lymph travels by itself. It is a derivative of the blood. As it washes the different tissues, cells draw out the nourishment they need and deposit their toxic waste to be carried away.

The Necessity of the Lymph System

One of the first indications of the importance of the lymph system is that it picks up toxic materials absorbed from the bowel wall. It takes the assimilated fats and other food particles from the villi of the small intestine and carries them throughout the body. Without all the proper chemical elements, our bodies cannot function. The lymph stream is the primary source of nutrients such as fatty acids, enzymes and prostaglandins, including the most gaseous and the most difficult to hold in solution (iodine, fluorine and chlorine).

The lymph fluid carries a great deal of sodium. The element sodium is an alkalinizing and a neutralizing element, often called the youth element. It is found in our saliva, in the walls of the gastrointestinal system and in the joint material.

We are supposed to secrete one quart of saliva per day from the parotid glands. They need exercise because they do not throw out saliva unless they are exercised. They are not exercised sufficiently unless we follow nature's call for raw food which necessitates vigorous chewing for an adequate period of time.

Sodium in the joints prevents the calcium in the lymph from depositing and causing spurs. Sodium in the lymph helps to neutralize acids, assists in the transport of some nutrients across cell membranes and replaces sodium used up in the gastrointestinal system walls, the joints and other parts of the body.

Hydrochloric acid is needed in the stomach to help digest proteins and to prepare calcium for absorption in the small intestine. Without

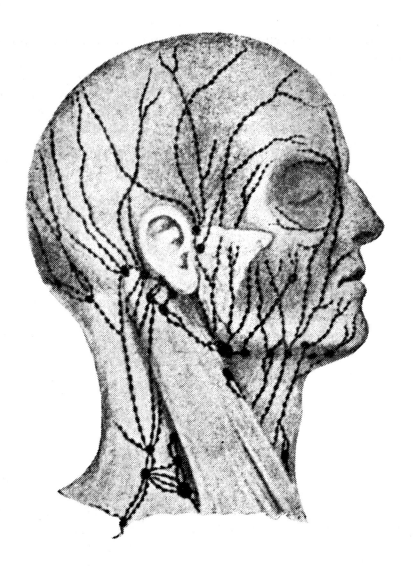

The network of lymph nodes and vessels in the neck and head. Lymph vessels ramify similarly throughout the body, and the little globular lymph glands in their course act as filters for waste products. Note that these glands are situated where they will receive squeezing action from the movement of muscles.

sodium in the stomach wall, the stomach does not secrete sodium properly.

Most people are deficient in hydrochloric acid. Reports indicate that 80% of the people over the age of 50 tested in hospitals lack adequate hydrochloric acid. By that, we know also that we lack sodium in the stomach wall. When the hydrochloric acid is finished with food in the stomach, food goes into the small intestine for further breakdown, digestion and assimilation. This is done by osmosis, which takes the digested food particles through the small intestinal wall and into the blood and lymph vessels. The nervous system governs the rate at which the bowel contents are moved along (which also depends on the amount of fiber in our food). The bowel pushes its contents along by wavelike movements called peristalsis.

If we do not use the right balance of foods in the first place, the lymph system is only going to take what it can. If it cannot get all the elements needed, it can only do a partial job of nourishing the body. Lymph fluid visits every cell in the body.

We need alkalinization; our blood is of an alkaline nature as is the lymph fluid. It is a sodium fluid. If we do not have the sodium in the stomach and bowel walls, we are not going to digest properly, and the lymph, being a sodium organ, will be deficient and unable to do its work properly.

The nervous system moves the foods to the small intestine after partial digestion in the stomach. The small intestine draws nutrients from the food we have ingested, as well as taking in the drugs we may use for the stomach (alkalinizers and baking soda). The villi in the small intestine work with whatever comes down the gullet, the stomach and into the small intestine, including drugs and pollutant chemicals that infiltrate the body through the lung structure. The bowel may also reabsorb toxic material from catarrhal discharges. Instead of allowing catarrh to be eliminated, it is reabsorbed back into the body. Then we expect the lymph stream to get rid of toxins and pick out only the good.

I believe that the lymph stream takes out that which is good and detoxifies as much of the toxic material as it possibly can. It cannot, however, remove all residues of drugs, fats from fried foods, cholesterol and toxic, acid byproducts of metabolism which it finally drops off in the various inherent weaknesses in the body or dumps in the bloodstream.

Lymph Nourishes and Cleanses the Body

We know that we take in nutrients from the small intestine, which, together with the stomach, processes everything that is put into the mouth. Without knowledge, wisdom and guidance, we cannot distinguish good food and drink from harmful or worthless food and drink. We are slaphappy in what we consume. We drink alcohol, smoke, use drugs and otherwise abuse the body, bringing so much toxic material into the body that the lymph stream is primarily occupied in detoxification and is greatly diminished in its ability to defend the body against bacterial or viral invasions. Besides, the blood (now acknowledged as an organ), cannot be any cleaner than what is taken into the digestive system. Similarly, the lymph stream cannot be any better than what it takes from the small intestine, to be delivered to various parts of the body.

There are additional health-related mental factors such as stress that affect the immune system. If a man works over at Ulcers, Inc., he lowers the effectiveness of his immune system. Another person says, "You make me sick to my stomach." The nervous system, the digestion and the bowel transit time are all involved in determining how well our immune system works and how efficient our lymph stream is at its job. The lymph can only work with what we feed it, and it is affected by how we take care of ourselves mentally, physically and spiritually.

The Large Bowel

The large bowel reabsorbs water and eliminates waste. Some B vitamins are absorbed through the wall of the large bowel, but so are toxins, especially when constipation and underactivity cause greater exposure to toxins for a longer time.

Here is where the nervous system comes in. A broken down nervous system, a fatigued or overwrought body does not eliminate properly. A person who is fed up with problems in the marriage and job is not going to have proper elimination. He is going to have difficulties in eliminating waste material from the bowel. In this sluggish elimination, the nerves to the bowel have been broken down and are underactive. The transit time is slowed (the transit time is the time it takes for elimination to take place, from the time food enters the mouth).

We don't answer nature's call. We develop pocketed conditions, diverticula due to putrefaction in an area of the bowel where there are inherent weaknesses in the tissue. Pocketed conditions develop where the toxic material in the pockets forms a source of infection. As we examine the neural arc reflex, we can see the direct effect of these bowel pockets upon different organs in the body.

When the iridologist examines the part of the iris named the autonomic nerve wreath, he may see an inherent weakness on the inside of the wreath, which "points to" another inherent weakness outside the wreath. This is an example of the reflex arc. A bowel pocket, indicated by the inner inherent weakness, is reflexly affecting an inherently weak organ outside the autonomic wreath, due to a genetically determined reflex relationship. This means that chronic bowel conditions can reflexly cause symptoms and disturbances elsewhere in the body, perhaps remote from the bowel.

We find that toxic material is absorbed by osmosis from an underactive bowel. Of course, most doctors do not believe that people can absorb toxic material from the bowel. They believe it is an eliminative organ that simply holds the toxic material until it is excreted. I have discovered, however, that bowel tissue is active and can release toxic material into the blood and lymph. The nervous system is not capable of overruling our decision not to answer nature's call for bowel elimination, and the bowel is forced to hold its contents. This is contrary to good health principles and can seriously compromise tissue integrity. When we don't answer nature's call, toxic material is absorbed in much greater amounts by the bowel.

The Lazy Bowel

A lazy bowel may develop over the years, in many cases due to the combined effects of a poor diet and bad bowel habits. The bowel tissue itself has a blood connection, a lymph connection and a nerve connection. And, blood, lymph and nerves reach every tissue of the body. The bowel wall is a very viable and soft tissue. As wastes pass through the bowel in the right amount of time, not much toxic material gets through the bowel wall. But when wastes are slowed down, the osmotic effect brings more toxic material from the bowel into the lymph and blood. The lymph and blood carry the toxic material throughout the body.

The Proof of the Pudding

Many times I have said that disease conditions develop in the body due to a toxic, underactive bowel. The proof of the pudding is shown in the results I have seen in my tissue cleansing program, a treatment taken by hundreds of patients and described in my book TISSUE CLEANSING THROUGH BOWEL MANAGEMENT.

Tissue cleansing only takes care of the bowel, but it is often followed by the disappearance of diseases in other parts of the body.

A Caucasus mountain man of the U.S.S.R. with Dr. Jensen.

The Lymph Stream — A Delivery System

We send messages by air, water and land; likewise, the body takes in chemical "messages" from polluted air, chemicalized water and various toxins from the land — such as residues of toxic pesticide sprays on the food we eat. Some of these chemicals feed our bodies and some are poisons. It is the chemical elements that we also take in drinks — vegetable juices, fruit juices, alcoholic drinks and commercial soft drinks — that the blood and lymph are going to eventually deliver to the organs in the body.

We are made of what we eat. We are what we digest, assimilate and absorb. If we could get the wisdom and knowledge of the foods that we should have and use foods properly, we would start developing great immunity to disease — but the problem starts in the blood and lymph streams.

Correlations with the Lymph Stream and Elimination

Some exudations that come from the body are putrid. The odor is anything but a clean odor. This means that elimination is being interfered with and is not being taken care of properly.

Today we are using suppressive methods to keep catarrhal exudates in the body. These catarrhal exudates are always found with great amounts of sodium fluid — the lymphatic fluids. The lymphatic fluids carry this waste and are at the bases of all boils, acne, pimples and other skin problems which involve elimination in which toxic materials are thrown out of the body.

I heard at one time that John Travolta would not sign his next movie contract if he had to use chemicals on his skin to improve his looks for camera and screen viewing. The skin is one of the main eliminative organs, and when the body odor beings to develop, it is because the lymph system is carrying too much toxic material to the skin. Not enough is being excreted by the other elimination channels.

Perspiration, if tasted, is salty, just as lymph fluid is salty. As lymph fluid comes to the surface of the skin, we eliminate salt. If we perspire profusely, we must take more sodium into our body in the form of foods rather than the inorganic salts many are using today.

We cannot use inorganic salt tablets. Inorganic salt is a drug and has side effects on the body. It produces more skin trouble, higher blood pressure and hardening of the arteries.

The lymph fluids can only distribute to the body what we eat. Here we have something to think about. We must recognize that toxic-laden lymph fluid is responsible for our tonsil troubles. The first operation we usually have is the tonsils. The tonsils are lymph tissues; here we deposit toxins carried by the lymph system, which enlarges the tonsils. Instead of taking care of the tonsil tissue by cleaning it out, we operate and take the tonsils out. The second operation generally is the appendix; this is also lymph tissue. When the lymph system no longer includes tonsils or appendix to dump its toxic wastes on; it has to find another outlet. So now the toxic materials are eliminated in the next inherent weaknesses in the body. We started with the first one and are now getting into the third, fourth and fifth.

The breasts, which are lymph tissue, may develop lumps, infections and tumors which must be cared for. But, what do we do? We operate, use radiation, chemotherapy and perhaps operate again. But no one is doing anything about cleaning up the lymph stream where the problem starts. We are not getting back to the basics in the care of our bodies as we should in order to have the best body possible so that the immune system is strengthened to resist and prevent disease.

We must realize that we have the opportunity to clean up the body and reverse our problems. We can straighten out our lives, our lifestyles and the paths we are following. We must recognize that the quality of our bodies is determined by what we eat, by our environment, by what is in our mind, by our spiritual endeavors and by the paths we take. As we follow the correct path, our lymph system will do its duty.

Doctors are saying that the lymph system is not doing its duty in many cases. It is time to cleanse and purify our bodies. I cannot help but think of Dr. Perrenon, who, during World War I, treated 500 sick sailors aboard the Kronprinz Wilhelm, a German warship that was out to sea nine months without fresh provisions, living on what they could raid from enemy ships. The health of the men gradually deteriorated until 500 of the sailors were unable to do their work. Their teeth became loose, their tongues turned black and bones broke at the least exertion. There were cases of pneumonia, pleurisy and rheumatism. The ship came into the James River on April 11, 1915, and anchored off Newport News, because too many of the men were breaking down. With no idea what was causing the problem, the German ship's physician, Dr. Perrenon, said, "Nature was not doing her duty." The German warship was able to come into a U.S. harbor peacefully in 1915, because the U.S. didn't declare war on Germany until 1917.

What was the problem on the Kronprinz Wilhelm? The officers and men were living on the food supplies from the ships they had been raiding. Why is it that not a single officer was sick? The officers took the fresh fruit and vegetables. The common sailors had steak, ham, cheese, white bread, canned milk, coffee and canned fruit and vegetables. The sailors were eating the preserved foods, and their bodies were gradually deteriorating and weakening. When they anchored in the U.S. port and were given whole cereal grains, fresh fruit and fresh vegetables, the German sailors quickly recovered.

The condition of the men aboard the Kronprinz Wilhelm was similar to what we have in civilization today. While it looks like nature is not doing her duty, the truth is we are not feeding the body right or treating it right. We are wearing it out early in life and we are trying to replace broken down organs by transplants for the heart and kidneys, for example. We are making artificial parts for the body to take the place of our natural parts. But we do not live in such a way that we can remain healthy.

Do you see that the beginning of our health problems is with how we live? Nature cannot do anything more than use what opportunity we give it. We can choose healthy living and right food programs, or we can ignore them. We cannot develop clean bodies with good immunity in the lymph system without right living.

Convalescent Homes

It would be an enlightening experience for you to visit some of the convalescent homes that are taking care of the elderly, the infirm and some who have chronic diseases. The people in these convalescent homes are not eating properly. If you visit people in these homes, you may encounter unpleasant body odors and the odor of urine from those who are not able to control their elimination. Besides eliminating in their protective pads or urinating in their beds, odors also come through the skin, breath, bronchial tubes and lung structures. Their lymph streams and all their eliminative organs are often overworked and toxic laden.

It is here where we must take a big look at the eliminative organs and what the lymph is doing. Some are using deodorants which just add a pleasant smell in the air to cover up other odors. The original odor has not left — it is a warning of what we should do. You should see the people who have gangrene setting in, tissue breaking down such conditions as boils, pimples, skin rashes and bed sores, because they cannot move or do not get the proper exercise. They are not eating the proper foods.

In many convalescent homes, patients receive cheap foods so the owners can make a better profit. These patients are not given whole grain cereals, vegetables, whole milk or fruit juices. They are given the cheapest of foods possible. The profit motive and good health care do not always go well together.

The way we treat our elderly is quite an indictment against our way of living today and the education we are given about nutrition. We cannot treat the elderly or infirm this way and expect them to have well bodies. When a person is at the point of being unable to move their body, they are on their way out.

Convalescent homes just keep people alive and seldom get them well. There is good nursing attention, but bad bodies are being nursed; they have bad digestive problems and bad elimination problems.

I have been in convalescent homes where patients had not had a bowel movement for two weeks. Some had never been given an enema. We do not recognize that lymph fluid throws off all the toxic material it possible can in all the elimination channels. The lymph fluid can only do what we can help it to and what we force it to do. It is only going to do its duty if we do our duty through a right-living process.

Our sense of smell is available to tell us when things are not right.

A gathering of Hunzakuts attending a court proceeding.

Dr. Jensen found very little brain anemia among the oldest Hunza people, as compared to the old people of other countries. The wool hats, Dr. Jensen believed, helped prevent the brain anemia by keeping their heads warm.

Another vigorous old man from the Caucasus mountains, over one hundred years old, with his one-year-old great-grandson. Again, notice the hat.

When we smell a ripe melon, we smell a beautiful scent. When we smell a ripe peach, we smell a beautiful scent. When we smell many different foods, their scents should be pleasant to us. But the smells in some convalescent homes are anything but pleasant — the odors from a sick person is anythings but pleasant. We must have cleanliness within before we can have cleanliness coming out of our bodies and cleanliness in our lymph systems.

Immunity in the Lymph System

We are finally coming down to the wire about the vital need to take care of our bodies. We are in the midst of a plague today and have come to the end of what our lymph system can do for us. It is being said that our lymph system is not doing its duty, but it seems more likely that we have forgotten our duty and our way along the path of wrong living. We have reached the point at which we no longer even think straight. We have lost sight of our duty to care for and feed our bodies right. We have lost the beauty which we know exists in this complex instrument of a million strings. We have forgotten the value of physical bodies made in the likeness of the Creator.

What are we doing? We are trying to live and be healthy on half a loaf of bread — half of the chemical elements needed by the body. We eat junk foods. We work too hard, play too hard. We are only half living the life that we should. This is the reason that half of the people are diseased today and the rest are only half as healthy as they should be. Unless we make a direct change in how we are living, we are not going to have good health or longevity.

Here is where we start at the beginning by cleansing the body, like our kids are saying today, "Come clean, man." It is time we recognize that we must clean up our act, change our association with bad foods, bad friends, bad habits and disease-oriented lifestyles. We must carefully consider the products and lifestyles advocated in the television we watch, the films we see and the magazines and books we read. Are we taking in life or death ideas?

We must educate ourselves and educate our children to set bad influences and habits aside and know from within that these things are not for us. They may tell you to say "no" to a junk food on occasion, without telling you what to put in its place. The desire for good health must be so strong in our consciousness that it is not going to be a big job to follow the right path to have the best of health.

Now What Do We Do About It?

The first thing we must do is take care of the digestive system with a program of foods and supplements giving us the chemical elements we need as well as stimulating better absorption of foods in the body. We must recognize that we cannot go through life without a positive mental outlook. It isn't only what we eat that builds a good body, but what we digest. An unhappy stomach cannot digest the foods properly. There are enzyme activities in the body which work best when we are happy. We cannot be well unless we are happy; likewise, we cannot be happy unless we are well. This, then, becomes a pathway, an education and something which we must learn.

If we digress or transgress, we must make it up the next day by going on juices and by being more careful than ever.

The first book to read to change your life and habits should be VIBRANT HEALTH FROM YOUR KITCHEN. You must have this. It is an education in itself and my best food work is in it. I believe in a balanced food regimen very much, and my approach to nutrition has changed the lives of thousands of people. Unless we go in this health direction, we cannot have a good lymph stream, a good blood stream, good tissue or better working and functioning organs in the body. This is the first program to start.

Those who are in a very serious condition, such as arthritis, psoriasis, asthma, high blood pressure, heart disease and other chronic diseases which are difficult to treat, should start at a deeper level. They should be reading my very important book, TISSUE CLEANSING THROUGH BOWEL MANAGEMENT. We cannot have a good body or a good lymph stream unless we have a clean, good-working bowel activity. Let me share a news note which was taken from the *Saturday Evening Post* a couple of years ago. Researchers at the University of California at San Francisco studied 1,481 non-nursing women. They found that women who had fewer than three bowel movements a week were five times more likely to have precancerous cells in their breast fluid than women who had bowel movements at least once a day. I want you to know that what happens in the bowel influences every cell in the body. If we are going to begin a clean program in life, we should start with a tissue cleansing program.

We should find out the various nutritional supplements which support the lymph system. The most important element is sodium. The sodium has burned out, used up or eliminated when one goes through the change of life with hot flashes and perspiration. This is when menopausal arthritis can develop from a lack of sodium.

Bill Walton, a professional basketball player, told me that he used to lose from ten to twelve pounds through perspiration in a single basketball game. How do we replace it? The fluid is replaced, but how about the sodium? What are the sodium foods and juices we should use? Celery is one of the finest sodium foods. Having celery juice along with carrot juice will give the natural cell salts we need to replace the salts lost in perspiration. We will then make our bodies clean from toxic material which must eventually be eliminated through juices.

We must cut out all drugs possible and eliminate them. Drugs have side effects, time-bomb effects and genetic effects. All side effects of drugs have a potentially bad effect on the body, and it is time we get rid of them. One of the finest supplements we can have is Sun Chlorella, which has an affinity for toxins and heavy metals, and carries them out in the catarrhal eliminations of our body. These eliminations have to take place in the body for a person to get well. We bring on what we call a healing crisis.

You should know what a healing crisis is. We must retrace our old problems and get rid of the white flour which has settled in our shoulder or the chocolate syrup which has settled in our knees. We have to have a good knee and we can have a good shoulder if we eat properly.

Our body is in constant change. For instance, we build new skin on the palm of our hands every 24 hours. If we do not like our bodies, we can change them, but we must put in new tissue to take the place of the old. If we don't change our habits, we are going to have the same body next week that we have right now. If things are not right, it is time for a change.

Another supplement you should consider is bee pollen, which is a whole food. I am trying to bring out the fact that if we can get into eating whole foods, we can make the best changes in the body with the vital trace minerals which we get in them. We do not get trace elements in foods grown in depleted soils.

The East African drought has come along to teach us a lesson. The people there are starving, and disease is preying on their under-nourished bodies. The United States is trying to help them over-come it by sending them white flour so they can make white bread or biscuits. White flour, however, will not build a good body. The East Africans will continue to be in this condition until they have the correct education to change it.

We have water shortages in many places in this country, and people are starting to recognize that no man can live on the soil without water. Many past civilizations have disappeared from a lack of water.

The plagues which have preceded AIDS are from a loss of im-munity which came from debauchery. The fall of the Roman Em-pire came due to their incorrect living. Today, we are treading the happy-go-lucky path. We are not learning the lessons of history.

We have a diseased civilization approaching. It is no wonder we are finding no cures when many people are not doing anything to improve their health but trying to get a kidney transplant so they can go on with their old lifestyle habits, alcohol and drugs and parties. Unless we see that we must have a healthy way of life 99% of the time, we will not make the grade.

AIDS is upon us. Cancer, cardiovascular disease and emphysema are upon us. The very worst diseases are upon us, and these ex-amples are all degenerative. Diverticula are upon us, found in the degenerative bowel areas. We have broken down the four elimina-tion channels more than any other parts of our bodies.

We have seen those who have had heart transplants die from kidney problems, pneumonia and bowel troubles. Barney Clark died from toxemia of the bowel. John Wayne, in the end, had cancer in the bowel. We die from conditions that are developing in the eliminative organs.

We cannot blame the lymph stream for this; the lymph always does its best with what we give it to work with. Now, we have to take care of what goes into the mouth and through out digestive system.

Here is the Big Lesson

The big lesson is to show that the digestive system is uniquely different from any other system in the body. Every organ depends upon our absorption and what we digest, what the villi are doing in the small intestine and what we absorb through the bowel wall through osmosis. Those who do not believe that we can absorb toxins through the bowel wall still have an interesting lesson to learn. They will find that as the bowel problems are taken care of, problems elsewhere in the body, distant from the bowel, will disappear. By the same token, organs develop diseases when we do not take care of the bowel.

It is the system outside of the body that causes most of our food problems today. This brings us back to Hippocrates' statement that doctors and others will never understand disease until they understand foods. Food should be our medicine, he said, and our medicine should be our food. Nutrition is the most neglected subject in the education of our doctors today, no matter what specialty they choose.

We Will Not Get Well with Treatments Alone

There is no profession that can get a person completely well putting new tissue in place of the old unless the proper diet is used. We can see changes in the tissues, but they are all temporary if we are going to depend upon treatments without adequate nutritional support. A temporary treatment is not going to have the lasting effect of putting in new tissue, a new knee or joint, five years or ten years from now. We are going downhill instead of uphill.

We can choose the privilege of going uphill by exchanging new tissue for old tissue that is not functioning properly. Nutrition and dietetics will make the changes we want in these tissues. Until the nurses and doctors become sick and turn to this approach to health, I doubt if we will have the changes necessary to educate our society. We are barely getting by; we are still able to crawl and get by on transplants, wheelchairs and crutches. This is the day to stop this. We have the privilege of making a new body if we will only try this new way of living.

There is Much Education Needed

There is much education needed. We must take care of our own health. What do we do between visits to the doctor? They make their living on our living! What are we going to eat for lunch? If it is not the proper thing, a symptom will follow one of these days, which will require attention from the doctor. Doctors have waiting rooms because they are waiting for you to become sick! How many waiting rooms are there for well people?

We have to change our system. We need a new breed of patients. This is the education program that I am trying to bring out. We should study nutrition. Doctors only study about fifteen to twenty hours in all the time they are in medical school. They have only learned how to take care of disease. They have not learned to take care of health! And this is the one thing that smothers disease. Disease cannot exist if we are chemically well balanced. At the bottom of every disease is a chemical imbalance.

It is a matter of knowing our nutrition. We must know the food sources where potassium is found. We must know how to build the lymph stream by following a good sodium program. We must learn our chemical elements. All this is possible.

I do not like to recommend my own books, but I wrote them for people just like you. I published them to educate people like you on better health. I am interested in mothers who can go through pregnancies to produce the best children possible for the next generation. Wives can keep their husbands on the job through well balanced meals. No woman should get married until she has a cookbook on healthful living; learning how to make nutritionally sound, as well as delicious meals is not going to kill anyone of us or rob us of the calcium we have in our bodies, as does white sugar. We need to know our food laws.

You have the privilege of following this program in my book, FOOD HEALING FOR MAN, which every person should read. Those who wish to take up nutritional work should also read my book THE CHEMISTRY OF MAN, to find out about chemical elements from the finest food sources possible. This book shows us what happens in the body when we do not have the proper chemical elements. These books were written to be a blessing to all; they were written with the hope that humanity could be better in the next generation than it is today.

This is all I can do. I want to be a blessing to you because I want to let you know that I really care about your health.

CHAPTER 8

UNDERSTANDING THE HEALING CRISIS

One of the greatest gifts Nature has bestowed upon man is the healing crisis, an upwelling of vital energy that casts off toxins, metabolic wastes and dead cells in an ailing body to make way for strong new healthy tissue. The human body was created to heal itself, provided Nature's laws are followed. Nature heals, but sometimes she needs a helping hand; and if we work with her, not against her, the healing comes. The healing crisis is Nature's way.

We find that the healing crisis is not a recent discovery. Hippocrates, the father of medicine, is credited with saying, "Give me a fever and I will cure any disease." For many centuries, physicians have realized that fever and purging of the body were essential, integral parts of the healing process. It was possibly not until the 19th century that homeopaths or nature cure doctors began to notice a distinct pattern in the healing process and named it the "healing crisis." Dr. Henry Lindlahr, early this century, paraphrased our earlier Hippocrates' quote, saying, "Give me a healing crisis and I will cure any disease.

Drugs and Symptoms

One of the greatest reasons I know to avoid the use of drugs is that they encumber the body, suppress symptoms and hinder the natural healing process from bringing the body to complete recovery. It is evident that people often "feel better" when they faithfully take their prescribed medication or some over-the-counter drugstore nostrum. Yet, we find that "feeling better" after taking a drug is seldom a reliable indication that the germ life or the chemical or neural process causing the symptoms, including pain and discomfort, has been blocked or neutralized in some way. This is not healing.

To truly understand disease, we must realize it consists of more than a set of symptoms. The symptoms are the body's alarm bells signaling that something is wrong. What creates symptoms? Irritated nerves, chemical imbalance, disturbance of brain function, metabolic changes in specific organs and other such processes. But what creates these processes? In some sense, all disease has its physical origin in tissue inflammation somewhere in the body. The cause may be traced further to an emotional reaction in the mind, a toxic substance from the environment or a shift in the body's metabolism such that cellular wastes are not being eliminated as fast as they are being formed. This condition is called autointoxication.

We find that Western medicine refers to the "invisible" early stage of any disease or ailment as the preclinical stage. That means they haven't found any way to show there is anything wrong yet. In the science of iridology, we use a different terminology because iridology — the analysis of tissue conditions in the body from reflex signs in the iris — is sensitive enough to detect early tissue changes.

Acute, Subacute, Chronic and Degenerative Conditions

The initial response of tissue to a source of irritation is to try to get rid of the cause by secreting mucus to protect itself and by relying on lymphocytes and antibodies from the natural immune system to kill or trap any foreign matter or germ life involved. The metabolism of the organ or tissue area may increase, and its temperature may rise in an effort to throw off the irritant. This we call the acute stage. The universal sign of this stage is catarrh, from the Greek words *cata rhein*, meaning "flow down."

If the acute stage is suppressed with pills, the tissue activity slows to what we call in iridology the subacute stage. The subacute stage is metabolically under normal, so the tissue begins to break down. Its resistance to the source of irritation is lowered. Cell wastes may build up locally, along with dead antibodies and germ life. Catarrh may begin to dry up in the tissue.

The chronic stage is often when clusters of symptoms become apparent, and it is at this stage that Western medicine usually provides a disease name for the condition. It may be asthma, arthritis, diabetes, cancer, heart disease or some other condition. The affected tissue is even more underactive at this stage, even less capable of defending itself, becoming more congested with toxic materials. An asthma attack, for example, is brought on when spasmodic contractions of the bronchial tubes try to eject the thick, dried catarrh and cellular toxic waste causing the problem. It is always unsuccessful (unless other steps are taken first.)

We refer to the most inactive stage of tissue as the degenerative stage. It is as close to being dead tissue as is possible while still having some detectable metabolic activity. It is usually saturated with toxic materials. This stage is almost hopeless.

So, we see there are four stages to disease in the perspective of iridology — acute, subacute, chronic and degenerative. The first stage is marked by hyperactivity and catarrh production. The second, third and fourth stages are characterized by progressive loss of vital function and, usually, accumulation of toxins. Weak tissue can't eliminate or resist toxic accumulations.

We will find that nature's way of healing is to reverse this process and throw off toxic accumulations in one or more healing crises, but before we get into the subject, we need to discuss what makes the body vulnerable to disease.

Constitutional Strength and Inherent Weaknesses

Doctors and even lay persons recognize that some people are more resistant to colds, ailments and disease than others. We say that such persons have strong constitutions. If we looked closely at some people's personal habits, we might find that their constitutional strength was average or below average, but they are taking above average care of their health — eating proper foods, getting adequate exercise and rest and getting out in the fresh air and sunshine. Their health may be better than those with strong constitutions who don't take proper care of themselves.

Most of us have inherited certain genetic traits from our family tree that give our bodies a mixture of inherent strengths and weaknesses. We might have a strong heart and strong kidneys, but a weak liver and bronchial tubes. Just as a chain is only as strong as its weakest link, the body is only as strong as its weakest organ or tissue area. Our inherent weaknesses are what make us vulnerable to ailments and diseases. How we treat our bodies actually determine whether we get those ailments and diseases or not.

We may describe inherent weaknesses and strengths in two ways. Structurally, inherently weak tissue is like coarsely woven burlap; inherently strong tissue is like silk — strong and finely woven. Coarse tissue can't hold nutrients and eliminate toxic wastes as well as fine, strong tissue. Another comparison is to point out that inherently weak tissue behaves as though it were slightly underactive in its metabolism. It absorbs nutrients less efficiently, operates at a lower energy and eliminates cellular waste more slowly than other tissue. Because of its lower activity level, inherently weak tissue may become a repository for drug residues, catarrh, heavy metals and other toxins.

I believe that the inherently weak organs, glands and tissues can be so well taken care of that we can lead healthy lives, just as healthy as those with strong constitutions. But we have to live wisely and avoid excess in lifestyle and personal habits.

I have observed, however, from the thousands of patients who have come to my sanitariums, that there are few who are wise enough to take care of their bodies properly. Inherently weak areas break down, and they come to see me. Very often, the breakdown is due to poor food habits.

Hering's Law of Cure

Constantine Hering was a European homeopathic physician who made a brilliant observation concerning the manner in which natural healing takes place. He wrote, "All cure comes from the head down, from the inside out and in reverse order as symptoms first appeared."

When we take this law apart and look at it carefully, we can see how ingenious it is.

How can cure come from the head down? In several ways. First, every organ, gland and tissue in the body is controlled and monitored by the brain. If the medulla is weak, there may be problems with the cardiovascular system, lungs or bronchials. We have to take care of the medulla before the chest organs will improve. Likewise, we must take care of the brain before any other organ, system or tissue can be expected to improve. Secondly, we find that every thought and emotion affect every cell in the body. If we are thinking destructive thoughts, they will affect our bodies. I believe we live on what we give forth, and if we give out anger, bitterness and hatred, our bodies will suffer for it. Studies have shown that negative thoughts contribute to disease, and positive thoughts contribute to health. We have to let go of criticism, backbiting and gossip. We have to look for the best in life and let the rest go. We have to love our enemies — not for their sake but for our own. I tell my patients they have to feel better before they can feel better. Do you understand? This is coming from the head down.

"Cure comes . . . from the inside out . . . ." The only way I know of to overcome disease and bring full healing is tissue renewal, tissue replacement. Every disease, every ailment, is characterized by tissue breakdown somewhere in the body. To overcome tissue breakdown requires that we assist the body in getting rid of the old and in making new tissue. We can't do that with drugs and medications. We can't do it with coffee, cigarettes and alcohol. We can't do it when we are working so hard that we are breaking down faster than we are building up. Healing is an inside job, and it starts at the cell level.

To start bringing cure "from the inside out," we go to the foods and supplements. Only foods can build new cells. We may need chiropractic to restore nerve function. We may need slant board exercises and Kneipp baths to bring up the blood circulation. But, unless, these therapies are used together with foods, tissue rejuvenation cannot take place. Our strategy is to take care of all nutrient deficiencies in the body, to build up overall strength until the body is capable of rebuilding damaged tissue in any place where tissue integrity has been compromised.

The gastrointestinal system is, to a great extent, the key to healing. Good digestion, good assimilation and good bowel elimination are essential, not only to healing but to good health maintenance. Eating proper foods does little good if they aren't digested or assimilated. And the best diet in the world will not be of much help to a person with a toxic, constipated bowel. So we must deal with digestion, assimilation and elimination to bring healing "from the inside out."

"Cure comes . . . in reverse order as symptoms first appeared." With this part of Hering's law, we find ourselves on the doorstep of the healing crisis. To get rid of a disease, we *reverse* the process by which we got it. We *retrace* the steps that led us to it. We don't "catch" diseases. We earn them. We eat and drink them into existence. So, we reverse the process. We work to earn good health. We eat right; we drink right; we get exercise and plenty of rest. And, in time, the body becomes strong enough to work its way back through old symptoms and get rid of their causes. This happens ". . . in reverse order as symptoms first appeared." I call this the reversal process.

Hering's law of cure is the roadmap we use to get to the healing crisis. I have sat by patient's bedsides spooning broth into their mouths a teaspoon at a time, and have seen them six months later —strong, cheerful, completely different people. Patients have come to me in wheelchairs and have left on their feet. I have taken care of thousands of "dropouts" from other doctors. I have seen Hering's law in action, and I have used it because it works with nature and not against it.

The Healing Crisis

The healing crisis is the high point of the reversal process, the destination we reach when we have successfully followed Hering's law. There is more to it than our brief description at the beginning of the chapter, and the wise person will learn to take delight when he recognizes the healing crisis coming. An example will illustrate.

Several years ago, a young man named Val came to me, 52 pounds overweight, his hands, feet, ankles and face swollen with edema. He had been given up to die by doctors at a Veteran's Administration hospital who told him he had an advanced case of glomerulo-nephritis (kidney disease), and there was nothing they could do for him.

I put him on a high protein, complex carbohydrate diet, along with a program of exercise, skin brushing, Kneipp baths, barefoot walks and hard physical work in the garden. He was determined to get well, and followed my directions completely. Normally, when a person has a toxic-laden body, I put him on juices to accelerate the cleansing, but this puts an extra burden on the kidneys. In Val's case, this would have been a mistake.

Working in the hot sun every day, perspiring, faithfully following this program, Val lost 32 pounds in a month's time. He felt wonderful. He looked wonderful. Then the healing crisis hit.

The big difference between a healing crisis and a disease crisis is that a healing crisis comes when a person is feeling on top of the world, while a disease crisis generally strikes when someone is tired, rundown, lacking in vitality. Val had brought his physical vitality up to the point where every organ of his body was supercharged and ready to work in harmony with the kidneys in getting rid of the toxic accumulations that had caused the kidney problems. For this young man, the first healing crisis came in a month; for others, it has taken longer — up to six months.

For three days, Val experienced a dramatic siege of diarrhea, having as many as 30 bowel movements per day. He lost 12 pounds before pulling out of it. Notice that the elimination took place primarily through the bowel, allowing the kidneys to rest. Afterward, he gained 4 pounds back.

Most healing crises last only a few days, but I have known of a few cases where they have gone longer. In healing crises, the patient reexperiences old symptoms — psychological as well as physiological symptoms — and this is entirely normal. There may be catarrh expelled from any or all of the body orifices once it has become liquefied in the body; no attempt should be made to suppress it. There may be fever, aches, pains, discharge from the eyes, skin eruptions, bronchial disturbances, headaches, itching, perspiration, vomiting, temporary swelling of the lymph nodes. All of this is a natural consequence of the body's expulsion of toxic material.

109

We cannot expect the body to become well overnight when a chronic disease has taken 20, 30 or 40 years to build up. It takes time to cleanse and rebuild tissue. I tell patients not to expect their bodies to be in relatively good condition in less than a year's time. For some, it is longer. In the meanwhile, there may be several more healing crises as the body continues on the reversal path.

For Val, the second healing crisis came about five months after the first. Going through another siege of diarrhea with considerable catarrh eliminated, he lost 10 pounds. A third healing crisis some months later brought vomiting and digestive upset. Physically, however, he was doing quite well.

To summarize Val's case, let's go back to Hering's law and look at a few comparisons. "All cure comes from the head down . . . ," it says. Val was determined to overcome his condition. His attitude was right. High protein meals, physical activity, hard work and Kneipp baths built up his nervous system and his blood circulation to the brain. The elimination of toxic material through the skin (perspiration) and the bowel, as well as the buildup of vitality through diet, took place "from the inside out." The healing crisis was proof that reversal was taking place in the body, and the symptoms came "in reverse order as they first appeared." No doubt, it was an underactive bowel that contributed to the kidney problems in the first place, and by toning and reactivating the bowel, the release of old toxins paved the way for the kidney tissue to rebuild and rejuvenate.

Notice that no attempt was made to specifically take care of the kidneys. I knew that the kidneys would not repair in a toxic body suffering from fatigue and low vitality, so the program I designed was aimed at cleansing and strengthening the body. Cleansing alone would not have revitalized Val's body. Strengthening along would have left the body too toxic for the kidney tissue to repair itself. We had to strike a balance between cleansing and strengthening to bring on a healing crisis.

For the great majority of people, cleansing out the bowel and taking on a positive outlook are key steps toward bringing on a healing crisis. My book *Tissue Cleansing Through Bowel Management* is aimed at helping those who wish to pursue the subject of tissue cleansing further.

After the Healing Crisis

As I have said many times, we build health just as we build disease. We have to work for it. We can't go through a healing crisis or two and return to our old ways, or we're begging for trouble.

We need to take a new path in life. We must eat better, exercise and get plenty of rest. We may have to change jobs if we've been working under too much stress. We may have to tackle the marriage problem to gain peace of mind. But, many have done it, and so can you.

CHAPTER 9

SELF SUGGESTION

The power of suggestion is the subconscious realization of an idea. Suggestion produced by an individual rather than another person is called self suggestion. Produced by the operator on the subject, it is called heterosuggestion.

We speak about waking suggestion, suggestively influencing a patient who is fully conscious. For suggestive results, it is necessary to have a certain degree of consciousness, but we have also seen unconscious suggestion used, about which the person is unaware. This type of suggestion is the most powerful.

Suggestion can also be realized by gestures and the appearance of the operator and may also proceed from a picture, sound or a color. The *special receptivity* for suggestions is called suggestibility.

The chief domain of suggestive therapy is: hysteria, neurasthenia and so-called today, psychasthenia.

Hysteria is abnormal physical reaction to psychic injuries, a psychosomatic reaction. It can imitate almost every disease, but the most characteristic hysterical symptoms are: Paralysis, convulsive phenomena, muscular spasms, pains and the like.

Through suggestive therapy, we can influence the symptoms of obsession, compulsion, phobias, anxiety, sexual dysfunction and other problems.

Symptoms which are mostly classed as neurasthenia (characterized by feeling of fatigue and exhaustion) are accessible to suggestive treatment. Here we find depressions, abulia, dyspesias, insomnia, disturbances of the bowel and bladder control, cardiac and other psychosomatic complaints.

The method of indirect suggestion includes the application of electric current, the placebo effect, special baths, etc.

The strongest suggestive action always proceeds from the *spoken word*, and depends upon the assured, decisive manner in which the suggestor moves and speaks.

The influence of mass suggestion can be used in practice in this way. A few patients sit in a quiet, dimly lighted room where there is only a blue light. Then the suggestor begins to speak softly in a monotone voice as follows:

You now breathe calmly, deeply and you feel how your muscles relax. . . How the heaviness flows through your body. . .You are now passing into the deep state of relaxation familiar to all of us just before we fall asleep at night. . .And now you remain in a dreamy condition, between sleeping and waking. . .Imagine now that I am speaking to your organs directly. . .to your liver. . .to your stomach. . .to your heart. . .to your brain. . .your glands. . .And now you feel confident that your healing and constructive forces start to work automatically so that all your organs function normally and regularly. . .And every day in every way you are getting better and better.

After these general suggestions, the doctor should allow the patient to remain in a state of relaxation. He goes from one to another, lays his hand on the patient's forehead, perhaps touches with the other hand the part affected, and whispers to a patient with special suggestions for him or her.

Application of Self Suggestion

The effect of self suggestion depends upon your state of relaxation. Therefore, the best time to perform self suggestion is in bed immediately before going to sleep. When you are completely

114

relaxed, repeat your previously-selected suggestive formulae about 20 times. After you have completed the practice of self suggestion, continue to relax until you fall asleep. Practice your suggestions at least a week before changing to new ones.

In the technique of self suggestion, the following rules must be applied:

1. The statement must be in *positive form*. Example: You must never say, "I am not nervous," but say, "My nerves become more strong, calm, resistant."

2. The formula must be *short*, in telegram style; the fewer words the better.

3. The formula should be *plastic*; that is, you should visualize everything that is contained in the formula. For example: "I can speak before many people with the greatest calmness and self confidence." Visualize in your mind how the people are under your influence and how you are calm, confident and at ease.

4. The formula should be repeated *quickly*, to avoid interference of other thoughts.

Suggestive Cards

One psychological aid that will keep your mind in a positive atmosphere without any conscious effort is the use of suggestive cards. You should distribute these cards in places where you most frequently look. Put one in your purse, one in your pocket, one in your drawer, one on your desk — places where you will be coming in contact with them and receiving the influence of the suggestion even unconsciously. They may look insignificant, but they are not intended to appeal to your conscious mind, therefore need no conscious attention. Continue using the cards until through these positive influences these attributes become your second nature. Copy onto cards any of the following self suggestions you wish to use:

Self Mastery. Whatever happens, I always remain calm, indifferent, self confident. Under all circumstances, I am objective, understanding, harmonious.

Success. Everything I do, I do every day better and better. Every day I am more courageous, confident, efficient.

Radiant Personality. I am free, independent, sure of myself. I am stable, cheerful, harmonious.

To Win Friends. I am interested in everything people like and do. I like to meet people and help others.

Inner Harmony. I am happy, satisfied and in good mood. In spite of disturbances, I always have inner harmony and peace of mind.

Others:

I am independent.

I am self confident.

I am alert.

I am stable.

I am harmonious.

I am freely expressing myself.

I am relaxed.

I am efficient.

I am energetic, courageous, self confident.

I am calm, restful, stable.

I am free, independent, responsible.

I work with concentration, enthusiasm, perseverance.

I am understanding, cooperative, harmonious.

I am indifferent to all wrong or negative influences.

Nothing and no one can disturb me.

Regardless of wrong ideas, I can continue to work, be constructive and creative.

I am in harmony with myself, with everything around me, and nothing brings me out of inner peace.

Self Suggestions from the Study of

Bernard Jensen Enterprises
24360 Old Wagon Road, Escondido, California 92027

SERENITY: My nerves are strong and calm. . .stronger and calmer. . .stronger and calmer. I feel in harmony with myself. . . with the universe. . .and with everything around me. . .I am rich with inner powers that give me harmony, security and serenity. . . Nothing, nobody can bring me out of unity with the Higher Powers. . .that protect me from all evils. . .and make me invincible, invulnerable, unshakeable.

NEW VITALITY: I feel full of health and the joy of living. There is sunshine in my soul today. The clouds have rolled away. . .and I feel confident, reassured and ever so contented. I feel young, ever so young. Every day in every way I feel younger and younger. I feel like a new and powerful personality, and can overcome everything with the greatest of ease. I feel wonderful. . .simply marvelous.

FOR YOUR GOOD HEALTH

Build a library of right living with Dr. Jensen's books, audio and video tapes, and attractive wall charts explaining the natural way to happy, healthy living. If they are not available in your local bookstore, write for our free catalog and price list to: Bernard Jensen International, Route 1, Box 52, Escondido, CA 92025.

Our Current Best Sellers!

Iridology: The Science and Practice in the Healing Arts, Volume II. Textbook, Practical Manual, Self-Study Course, Exhaustive Reference Work. Send for our free color brochure.

Iridology Simplified. Introduction to the Science of Iridology and its relation to Nutrition. Ideal for the beginner — color pictures, charts, case histories, 38 pages.

Tissue Cleansing Through Bowel Management, including the Ultimate Tissue Cleansing Program. Illustrated, 179 pages.

Arthritis, Rheumatism and Osteoporosis. An effective program for correction through nutrition. Special diets, supplements, drinks and exercises.

Vibrant Health From Your Kitchen. Teaches basics of nutrition. Food guide for family health and well-being.

Chlorella: Gem of the Orient. Dynamic food discovery for health and healing. Build immunity while repairing your body.

Breath Again Naturally — How to Deal with Catarrh, Bronchitis, Asthma — by managing lung and bronchial conditions through a natural living and eating program. Illustrated, 128 pages.

Food Healing for Man — A wonderful primer of nutrition and food facts for everyone, especially for those starting out in the nutrition field, exploring the role of deficiencies in disease and the restorative power of a balanced food regimen.

The Healing Mind of Man — Wholistic healing principles for the body, mind and spirit, including the roles of inspiration, wisdom, peace and beauty in healing. The many stories from Dr. Jensen's experience will uplift and delight readers.

The Chemistry of Man. In-depth study for the serious student of chemicals in soil and foods. To know disease we must first know the value of foods. We mold to the food we eat.

NEW BOOKS NOW AVAILABLE:

The Master Feeding Program. A wonderful compendium of Dr. Jensen's food ideas, starting with his thesis that nutritional deficiencies are at the root of human disease and ending with a balanced food regimen for preventing or reversing disease.

Herbal Handbook. An invaluable guide to herbs for each stage of many diseases. Recipes, and how to plant your own herbal garden.

Dr. Jensen's Favorite Exercises. You'll learn about figure-eight exercises, slant boards, rebounder and eye exercises, and the importance of skin care.

The Greatest Story I Have Ever Told. An easily understood narrative concerning what iridology is, how it works, what it does and how its use in the drugless healing arts could increase the effectiveness of other therapies, especially when used in combination with nutrition.

People Affinities. A book for everyone who would like to understand more about what makes relationships work and what we can do to have better relationships.

Home Wellness Center. How to convert your home into a "Wellness Center" by considering your home in a wholistic way and by making practical changes in your home life where many of our health problems begin.

Rejuvenation and Regeneration. Nature's way of healing, the healing crisis, the reversal process, and how it works are all discussed.

Color, Music and Vibration. Dr. Jensen discusses the many ways in which color, music and sound influence our lives and our health. Discover how the color of foods stimulate different responses in the body.

Soil and Immunity. The relationship between soil and health. Learn the whys and hows of soil care, including composting, value of worms, importance of bioorganic soil treatment, and the dangers of inorganic chemical fertilizers and pesticides.

Love, Sex and Nutrition. When we realize that both love and sex involve wonderfully intricate flows of energy and body chemistry, we also realize that good nutrition is as necessary to healthy relationships as to physical health. You'll love this book!

In Search of Shangri-la — A Personal Journey to Tibet. Dr. Jensen's 1986 visit to Tibet and Lhasa, long-called "the forbidden city," not only unfolds as an exciting travel adventure but a spiritual journey as well.

Beyond Basic Health: Advanced Thinking for the Healing Arts. Dr. Jensen shares his view of how iridology and nutrition can be used to greatly increase the effectiveness of patient health care in all drugless health arts.

Foods That Heal. Three perspectives on the healing power of foods start off this narrative: Hippocrates, V.G. Rocine and Dr. Bernard Jensen. The second half is a fascinating food encyclopedia, giving the history and therapeutic value of many fruits and vegetables.

The Spoken Word of Dr. Jensen

Dr. Jensen's entire Nutrition Course is available on audio tape: **Nutrition I, Nutrition II** and **Clinical Nutrition,** each set 10 hours.

Three latest tapes: **Food Healing for Man, Nutrition for Longevity** and **Nutrition for Youth.**

Video Tapes

Latest releases: **An Enchanted Evening in Color; In Search of Shangri-la — A Personal Journey to Tibet;** and **Hunza: Valley of Health and Long Life.**

Tissue Cleansing — Three hours of Dr. Jensen's teachings on colon health, so important in today's world.

Charts

Beautiful color charts on Iridology, Body Systems, Nervous System, Vitamins-Minerals-Herbs.

For further information on other books, audio and video tapes and prices, contact your local health food store or write to:

Bernard Jensen Enterprises
24360 Old Wagon Road, Escondido, California 92027